GREATEST GAMES
SUNDERLAND

ROB MASON

GREATEST GAMES
SUNDERLAND

ROB MASON

Published by **Know the Score Books** (2010) in association with Sunderland AFC

Know The Score Books is an imprint of **Pitch Publishing**

Pitch Publishing
A2 Yeoman Gate
YeomanWay
Durrington
BN13 3QZ

www.pitchpublishing.co.uk
www.knowthescorebooks.com

Text © Rob Mason 2010

Rob Mason asserts the moral right to be identified as the author of this work.

A CIP catalogue record for this book is available from the British Library.

ISBN: 978-1-84818-204-2

Printed and bound in Great Britain by The CPI Group

CONTENTS

DEDICATION

This book is dedicated to my brother
Gordon Mason. Whereas the first time I
saw Sunderland they won 7-1 and I was
hooked, Gordon's first game was a dismal
1-0 home second division defeat by
Oxford in 1970 when he was just six.
Nonetheless he is every bit as keen as any
supporter as are his wife Debra and
children Jonathan and Rebecca.

FOREWORD

Gary Rowell scored 103 goals for Sunderland, many of them from midfield. Rowell was a clinical finisher who often saw chances no one else realised were even there and possessed the precious gift of being in the right place at the right time. He was also quite possibly the best penalty taker in the club's history, scoring 20 out of 21. In 2010 Sunderland supporters still sing of 'Living in a Gary Rowell World' at just about every game.

I HAVE MANY vivid memories of my playing days and treasure every one of my appearances and each of my goals. I've always been a Sunderland supporter and deeply appreciate how fortunate I was to be able to play for my team. Sunderland is a truly great football club with a very long and proud history. As a young boy coming through the ranks when the FA Cup was won in 1973 I looked up to those players and still do to this day. For me to come into the team a few years later and play alongside the likes of Bobby Kerr, Billy Hughes, Vic Halom, Dick Malone and Monty was an incredible thrill.

There were some great times in my 297 games for the club. Of course everyone remembers me for my hat-trick when we won 4-1 away to Newcastle in 1979 and what amazes me is that so many people come up to ask me about that game when they weren't even born then. The stories are passed down the generations though and that's where this book of *Sunderland's Greatest Games* is so enjoyable in that it lets you re-live your greatest days as a supporter and lets you find out about the games and the players you've heard about.

Whenever I'm reminded that along with the great Len Shackleton and Kevin Phillips I'm one of only three people to score 100 goals for Sunderland since the war I'm honoured to be in such company. I realise that I'm so lucky in that as the only one of the three to have grown up a Sunderland supporter I've been blessed in having scored more goals for the club than anyone else who was a lifelong Sunderland fan since the times of Raich Carter and Bobby Gurney in the 1930s.

I still see every Sunderland game now both home and away as summariser for Real Radio and I still will the team on as much as every fan, as much as I did when I first went to the match as a kid and as much as I did when I was playing. Sunderland does that to you.

GARY ROWELL

FOREWORD

Gary Bennett is the fifth-highest appearance maker in Sunderland's history. Three of his 443 appearances for the club were at Wembley: the 1985 League Cup final, the 1990 play-off final, the 1992 FA Cup final and he was also part of the squad for the 1988 League Centenary tournament. Although he was a defender Gary also scored many memorable goals such as his dramatic play-off goal against Gillingham, his goal against his first club Manchester City on the final day of the 1990/91 season, his sublime last-minute winner against Manchester United at the start of that season and beating Peter Shilton just two minutes into his debut back in 1985. 'Benno' endeared himself to the fans with his total commitment and in 2010 as a match summariser for the BBC he is still someone who lives and breathes SAFC.

F ROM THE moment I made my debut for Sunderland I knew I had come somewhere special, somewhere where football means everything. I played a lot of games for the club and quickly learned that first and foremost the supporters wanted to see you getting stuck in and giving everything you had. That's only right and I made sure that I always tried as hard as every supporter would have done if they'd been able to play. As long as you do that at Sunderland the fans will stick by you and if you don't do that you shouldn't be wearing a Sunderland shirt.

I was fortunate to play in some great games in my time at the club including seven of the ones in this book. We had some terrific wins and some days where things didn't go our way. I played just when the play-off system was starting and experienced the highs and lows, there were promotions, relegations and cup finals, everything except a dull moment really.

I'm still at every game, working for the BBC and frequently get people coming up to me wanting to talk about games, goals and the characters behind them. I expect everyone who has either supported the Lads for a long time or someone just starting to follow them now will find *Sunderland's Greatest Games* lets them re-live some of the best games they've been to or heard about. I was lucky to play a part in some of them and lucky to have played for a club where once you are red and white you are always red and white.

GARY BENNETT

INTRODUCTION

CHOOSING SUNDERLAND'S greatest games is of course a difficult task. Picking the big cup games and the most important derby victories is the easy bit. The hard part is deciding which games to leave out. No doubt there'll be plenty who will argue I should have found room for such and such a game that isn't here. Maybe the 6-4 FA Cup defeat at Everton in 1935 that many on Merseyside claim is the greatest game ever seen at Goodison Park should have been included or perhaps the 1895 club record 11-1 FA Cup win over non-league Fairfield? Of more recent vintage maybe the 5-0 Premier League away win at Derby in 1999 complete with a Kevin Phillips hat-trick should have been included or perhaps the game at the same ground four years later when goalkeeper Mart Poom sensationally headed a fantastic injury time equaliser.

The fact that famous occasions such as these didn't make the cut indicates that the 50 fixtures that are featured are all great games. The book goes right back to 1892 and right up to 2010. The game that sealed each one of Sunderland's six top flight titles is featured as are all four of the Lads' FA Cup finals. The back to back 2-1s at Newcastle are here as is the Gary Rowell hat-trick of 1979 and the all time top flight record away win of 9-1 at Newcastle in 1908. The biggest games of the glorious 1973 cup campaign are here as is the pinnacle of the Peter Reid years – the 4-1 over Chelsea when SuperKev and Niall Quinn were unstoppable.

For all of these, *Sunderland's Greatest Games* doesn't just tell you what happened in the match. Each game is put into context with an explanation as to what made the match so important and many of the featured games include first hand comments from those who took part.

Niall Quinn played in seven of the greatest games and has been chairman in three more. With Sunderland looking to get back to the days when they were an accepted part of the top half of the top flight there is reason for Sunderland supporters to believe that there are many more great games to come in the next few seasons. Knowing all about Sunderland's greatest games of the past can only help you to appreciate the great games that are yet to come even more.

Rob Mason

ACKNOWLEDGEMENTS

THANKS TO Mike Gibson for help with checking facts especially for matches from the Victorian era and to Barry Jackson especially for help with details on the use of substitutes. Thanks also to Jack Mitton for help with referee's names. Thank you especially to my wife Barbara Mason who as well as helping with research also gets the job of checking everything. Although her visits to the match are occasional ones she increasingly finds herself an expert on players of the 1890s to date, not least from walking past pictures of 'The Team of All The Talents' everyday when she climbs the stairs at home!

Finally thanks to every player who has contributed to this book and especially to the 'Great Garys', both Rowell and Bennett who have each kindly provided a foreword for the book. As players who made 740 appearances for Sunderland between them and both scored some vital goals featured in this book they already hold a special part in Sunderland's history. As long-standing summarisers for Sunderland AFC's two commentary partners BBC Newcastle and Real Radio, they both still attend every match and from sitting near them in the press box I can vouch for the fact that they are both still as passionate about all things red and white as when they were playing.

v Blackburn Rovers 6-1

Newcastle Road, The Football League
April 16th 1892. Attendance: 10,000

SUNDERLAND	BLACKBURN R	REFEREE
Doig	Arthur	Mr. R.H. Lythgoe,
Porteous	McKeown	Liverpool
Gow	Forbes	
Wilson	Almond	
Gibson	Dewar	
Murray	Stringfellow	
Hannah J.	Walton	
Smith	Campbell	
Campbell	Cockshutt	
Millar	Hall	
Hannah D.	Chippendale	

SUNDERLAND CLINCHED their first ever league title with this handsome victory to climax only their second ever season in the league. It was the last year of the four-year-old Football League being made up of a single 'table', a meeting at The Queen's Hotel in

*The Queen's Hotel, Fawcett St. Sunderland is where the
second division was created.*

Sunderland during the summer of 1892 created the formation of the 'Second Division' which began the following season and so when Sunderland retained their title they became the first ever winners of 'Division One' just as they'd been the last winners of 'The Football League'.

Thrashing Blackburn before a capacity crowd at the Newcastle Road ground to seal the title was the perfect way in which to establish Sunderland as the finest club in the country. It began a four year period when Sunderland were champions three times and runners-up once, no wonder they were called 'The Team of All The Talents'.

Blackburn were a glamour side of the day. They weren't any great shakes in the league but had won the FA Cup in the last two seasons having begun the first of those campaigns by knocking Sunderland out of their last FA Cup tie before becoming a Football League club. Indeed Blackburn Rovers had won the FA Cup in five of the last eight years.

Sunderland had swept all before them at home. Going into this final home fixture they had won all twelve league games as well as both home cup ties. The first goal Sunderland would score in this game would be their 50th at home in the league that season while less than a goal a game had been conceded in the Newcastle Road fortress. There had though been five defeats on the road, one at Rovers' Ewood Park in early November since when Sunderland had won all thirteen league games – a club record that still stands – until the week before Rovers' visit when Notts County had inflicted a 1-0 defeat. Were Sunderland going to fall at the final fence? Had nerves taken over? Would Sunderland come unstuck on the verge of success as they would do several times in the years to come, not least in 1903, 1950 and 1963 to name but three?

Any early nerves were quickly put to rest though as Johnny Campbell gave Sunderland the lead after just eight minutes, finishing off a John Smith (in his final league or cup game for the club) cross with the aplomb you'd expect of a man who scored 24 more goals for the Lads than Kevin Phillips – in 20 games less. However Rovers

Johnny Campbell scored four times.

weren't to let Sunderland have things all their own way early on and made a game of it eventually levelling before half-time when Coomb Hall headed past legendary home keeper Ted Doig. Stung by the equaliser the home side restored their lead straight away through the other great goalscorer of the era, Jimmy Millar, who headed home a centre from captain Hugh Wilson.

Determined not to leave themselves open to a second equaliser, Tom Watson's side attempted to take the game away from the visitors who with the help of the frame of the goal, which Sunderland struck three times in the first half, held on until shortly before the break when Campbell gave Sunderland a cushion of a two-goal lead with his second of the game (although some reports credit this goal to David Hannah).

Sunderland were now cruising. Since the 3-1 reverse at Blackburn almost six months earlier only Accrington had scored more than one goal against Sunderland in the league, and they'd still lost on their own patch. The team took to the field for the second half with one hand already on the Football League Championship trophy and proceeded to play like champions, Campbell heading home two corners to give him four goals in the match. The visitors again needed the woodwork to rescue them and deny the imperious Wilson a goal but the icing was put on the cake two minutes from time when Jimmy 'Blood' Hannah got on the score-sheet.

Sunderland celebrated by rubbing the noses of rivals Sunderland Albion into the ground. Formed by Sunderland's disgruntled founder James Allan as a rival club back at Sunderland's first home of the Blue House Field in Hendon, Albion were given the same treatment as Blackburn and beaten 6-1 in a friendly 48 hours after Sunderland became champions of England for the first time. Sunderland had delivered the knock-out blow to the rivalry between the clubs. They were champions of the country, winners of a league Albion could only dream of being part of and ready to dominate the world of football in such a manner that Sunderland would indelibly print its name on the game as one of the country's truly great clubs. In 2010 only Manchester United, Liverpool, Arsenal, Everton and Aston Villa can claim more titles than Sunderland. This first title established Sunderland amongst the game's giants.

v Burnley 3-2

Turf Moor

April 15th 1893. Attendance: 10,000

SUNDERLAND	BURNLEY	REFEREE
Doig	Hillmann	Mr. T. I. Robson,
Porteous	Nicoll	Birmingham
Gibson	Lang	
Wilson	Mullineux	
Auld	Espie	
Dunlop	Livingstone	
Hannah J.	Crabtree	
Harvie	Buchannan	
Campbell	Turnbull	
Millar	Bowes	
Scott	Hill	

THIS WAS Sunderland's third season in the Football League. Opponents Burnley had already featured strongly. They had been the visitors to the Newcastle Road ground for Sunderland's first ever league game in 1890, winning 3-2 and Sunderland had completed their second season at Turf Moor having already won the title. This match was the final one of the 1892/93 season. Sunderland had already sealed the retention of their status as champions but had another aim in mind. 'The Team of All The Talents' required three goals to become the first ever team to score 100 league goals in a season. Not bad when you consider the season consisted of just 30 games!

West Brom had been walloped 8-1, Accrington had been hit for six on the opening day while Aston Villa had had half a dozen put past them both home and away. Newton Heath (or Manchester United as they are now) had been hammered 6-0, one better than the five they'd been beaten by on their own ground. Five had also been put past Wolves, Nottingham Forest and Blackburn Rovers while Royal Arsenal had been outgunned 6-0 in the cup just for good measure. This team weren't called 'The Team of All The Talents' for nothing and they badly wanted that century of goals.

Four Sunderland players had reached double figures in the seasonal goal-scoring stakes, the top scorer being Johnny Campbell who notched 30 in his 27 appearances but it was Campbell's ex Renton teammate John Harvie who came good in this match. At only 5'4" he was the same height as Bobby Kerr who would be the smallest FA Cup final captain when he led Sunderland to victory in 1973 and he scored twice in this match, almost doubling his tally for the year. Once Harvie put the Lads ahead from a 20th minute free kick, Sunderland tore into the home side, soon doubling their lead this time through Hugh Wilson, the man who would eventually succeed John Auld as captain although some contemporary reports attributed this goal to Campbell.

Sunderland's players weren't too concerned who scored the goals just so long as the team reached the magical 100 mark. Goal celebrations are considered a modern phenomenon. Ripping your shirt off these days constitutes a yellow card while somersaults, having a boxing match with the corner flag, running away pointing a finger of each hand to the skies in tribute to your deceased mother and all kinds of rehearsed training ground routines are now commonplace. In Victorian times it was assumed that a goal might be greeted by a manly handshake and perhaps a slap on the back for the scorer. By all accounts while the first two goals were celebrated in typically modest fashion, when Harvie scored again the change from 2-0 to 3-0 and with it the whirring round of a third digit in the goals for column for the first time of any team ever, resulted in the players performing cartwheels such was their delight at having achieved the century.

Perhaps the Wearsiders were still giddy from the celebrations of John Harvie's goal as Burnley fought their way back into the match. A warning shot was fired when Nicholl beat Sunderland's illustrious goalkeeper Ted Doig only for the 'goal' to be disallowed for offside. From a Sunderland point of view it was just as well the goal was ruled out as the Clarets were to score twice, the first from a tremendous shot from Crabtree that left Doig helpless to make the score 1-3 with half an hour to play.

Hugh Wilson later took over from John Auld as the captain of 'The Team of All The Talents'.

Burnley had the wind behind them in the second half and continued to push Sunderland back. With the 100 goal mark reached and the title already won by a country mile, Tom Watson's side maybe took their foot off the pedal because the Clarets were to further reduce the deficit through Bowes. By this time Sunderland were down to ten men, full back William Gibson having had to retire through injury.

Though Burnley pressed hard for an equaliser Sunderland dug in to show that being the 'Team of **ALL** The Talents' they could defend too and held out to finish the season with a win.

Impressed by that century of goals? One more and Sunderland would have totalled 200 that season if cup goals and goals scored in the 26 friendly matches 'The Team of All The Talents' played that season are included! These additional games included a 6-2 win away to Glasgow Rangers and a 6-1 February triumph over Newcastle on their own soil. What a team!

Ted Doig

3 v Everton 2-1

Newcastle Road, Division One
April 20th 1895. Attendance: 20,000

SUNDERLAND	EVERTON	REFEREE
Doig	Hillman	Mr. J. H. Strawson,
McNeill	Kelso	Lincoln
Gow	Arridge	
Dunlop	Boyle	
McCreadie	Holt	
Johnston	Stewart	
Gillespie	Williams	
Harvie	Bell	
Campbell	Hartley	
Millar	Chadwick	
Hannah J.	Milward	

SUNDERLAND ENTERTAINED second-placed Everton with 20,000 at the Newcastle Road ground where the gates opened two hours ahead of the 4.00pm kick-off. It was only the third time this many supporters had squashed into the venue Sunderland had played at for nine years. As yet Newcastle, who might be expected to draw a big crowd, had yet to reach the top flight of English football which Sunderland were dominating to the extent that with this victory they became the first ever club to be champions of England for a third time.

Going into the game Sunderland had won their three previous league games all away from home to maintain their place at the top of the table, a position they'd held since New Year's Day. The Toffees in contrast had slipped up, losing at home to lowly Derby the previous week. Everton had to win on Wearside to have a chance of stealing past Sunderland. In looking to win their second title – the first having been in Sunderland's first season as a league club in 1890/91 – Everton were seeking the championship in what was bottom-of-the-table Liverpool's first season at the top level. This was the red and white's final game whereas Everton still had to face third-placed Aston Villa. If Everton could win their final two matches they would draw level with Sunderland on points and depending upon the margin of victory could overtake the Lads on goal average.

The teams had played out a 2-2 draw at Goodison Park earlier in the season when Everton topped the table. Sunderland were fourth at the time but Everton lost more than a point to a rival that day when two goals from Jimmy Millar brought the Lads level having been two down. Everton's captain was centre forward Jack Southworth who had been the country's leading scorer the previous season. He had nine goals from nine games of which Everton had won eight but the England international sustained a serious injury against Sunderland which prematurely ended his career.

Sunderland were missing skipper Hugh Wilson when Everton came to the north east but had a largely settled side, goalie Ted Doig and centre forward Johnny Campbell maintaining their ever present record by playing while five others had barely missed a game.

Campbell was the first to threaten, forcing Jack Hillman into a save from distance. Johnston and Harvie then combined to create an opening for winger Hannah who outstripped Stewart and Arridge only to shoot well over. Hannah was seeing plenty of the ball and won a corner before McCreadie again tested Hillman.

Everton got forward for the first time thanks to good work from Williams and Bell, the latter crossing for Millward to bring a good save out of Doig at the cost of a corner duly cleared by Gow. It was end to end stuff as Hillman made a great save from a low effort from Dunlop which he did well to scoop around the post for a corner.

The Everton keeper had been Burnley's custodian when Sunderland took the title at Turf Moor two years earlier and was playing like a man possessed as he looked to get the better of the Wearsiders this time, next rushing out of his goal to hack clear as Hannah again broke clear of the Everton defence.

Everton enjoyed a good spell which saw Bell have a 'goal' disallowed for offside after great work by Chadwick and Millward before Sunderland had another let-off when Boyle hit the bar.

Sunderland weathered the storm and gradually got on top, Hannah bringing a full-length save out of Hillman who was then beaten by Campbell only for the Sunderland man to be ruled offside.

The breakthrough arrived ten minutes before half-time and it came from a dead ball. Fouled by Holt, Millar took the free kick he'd won himself, teeing the ball up for Andrew McCreadie to power home. Almost immediately Hillman made a 'grand save' from Millar and Everton responded, Williams forcing Doig into an equally impressive stop to protect Sunderland's narrow half-time advantage.

The early stages of the second half were even but with everything to play for 'The Men from the Hill Country', as Everton were known during the Victorian era, pushed Sunderland back and brought the score level with a 55th-minute goal from Edgar Chadwick who deceived Doig with a low shot from long distance having taken a pass from John Bell.

Nothing less than a win was good enough for Everton and they remained on top for the next 20 minutes during which Sunderland had their backs to the wall as they tried to satisfy the big crowd. Against the run of play Sunderland scored the decisive goal with quarter of an hour remaining. Full back Donald Gow was one of

The famous Thomas Hemy painting of the Newcastle Road ground in 1895 – this image is from a January meeting with Aston Villa.

Donald Gow

several Scottish stalwarts in the side, a speedy, strong player who gave the team good service as well as sporting a magnificent moustache. It was Gow who walloped a hefty clearance that sent James 'Blood' Hannah clear.

No relation to David Hannah who played for Sunderland during the same era, 'Blood' had made his debut against Everton four years earlier after joining from the rival Sunderland Albion. A speedy Scot, Hannah raced forward to score one of the most important of his 75 goals for Sunderland. Needing two goals in the closing stages, Everton's challenge fell away as Sunderland held out for their 21st victory in 30 games. 'The Team of All The Talents' were champions again.

v **Newton Heath** 2-0

Newcastle Road, 'Test Match'
April 26th 1897. Attendance: 8,000

SUNDERLAND	NEWTON HEATH	REFEREE
Doig	Barrett	Mr. T. Helme,
McNeill	Doughty	Farnsworth
Gow	Errentz	
Ferguson	Draycott	
McAllister	Jenkyns	
Wilson H.	McNaught	
Gillespie J.	Bryant	
Harvie	Donaldson	
Morgan	Boyd	
Hannah J.	Gillespie M.	
Campbell	Cassidy	

FOR 'TEST MATCH' read play-off. Two words that strike dread into the hearts of Sunderland supporters who have endured the 1998 play-off defeat on penalties at Wembley, the trauma of sinking into the third division on away goals in 1987 despite identical score-lines home and away over 90 minutes and the 2004 defeat on penalties against Palace. Even when successful in 1990, after brilliantly beating the Magpies at the semi-final stage, Sunderland supporters suffered lame defeat to Swindon in the Wembley final only to find the club subsequently promoted courtesy of a meeting some weeks later. Play offs then do not have a happy place in the psyche of the red and white army.

Consider that the trials and tribulations of the play-offs of the modern era have come at a time when Sunderland supporters were used to expecting the worst on such occasions, whereas when in 1897 Sunderland found themselves facing the club that five years later would become Manchester United in the play-offs – or 'Test Matches' as they were then called – it came as a massive shock to the system. Sunderland had been as dominant as Manchester United themselves have been in the modern era. Imagine Rooney and Rio in a relegation scrap and you begin to get the picture of what it meant for 'The Team of All The Talents' to play in this game.

A year earlier Sunderland had finished a creditable joint fourth though this was a great disappointment to a crowd who had welcomed three league titles in the previous four seasons, having to make do with runners-up spot on the other occasion. 1896/97 had been a shock on a par with seeing Bigg Market phone boxes survive a Tyneside derby defeat a century later. There had been little to warn supporters. 1895/96 had ended with six victories in the final seven league games but no wins in the first eight games of the new season brought only three draws and a failure to score in five of those matches dumping Sunderland firmly at the foot of the table.

What was missing was manager/secretary Tom Watson. He had taken a big pay rise in the summer to join newly promoted Liverpool leaving Robert Campbell, the half brother of Sunderland forward Johnny Campbell, in charge on Wearside. Robert could have done with Johnny banging a few goals in but while he'd scored over 150 times in the previous six seasons, this dreadful year he could only manage a measly four despite playing in all but one of the 30 league fixtures. Johnny Campbell though wasn't the only member of 'The Team of All The Talents' whose talents were on the wane. He was one of five players who had given the club magnificent service for whom the Newton Heath 'Test Match' was their final game.

The 'Talents' thankfully could still summon up reserves of energy on special occasions. They'd shown this in January when after a run of one win in ten they lifted themselves off the bottom of the table by scoring four goals to beat eventual runaway champions Aston Villa. Another of the 'Talents', James Gillespie, bidding farewell against Newton Heath, had scored twice to beat Villa and it would be he who came up trumps again in Sunderland's hour of need.

Like the first play-offs of the modern era, the 'Test Matches' involved teams from the bottom of one division and the top of another to determine who would play at the higher level the following season. Thus second-bottom Sunderland and back markers

The Newcastle Road ground in 1897 when the 'Test Match' with Newton Heath was played. Note the pitch markings of the time.

Burnley played the top two of the second division (Notts County and Newton Heath) home and away, the two sides with the best records claiming the two top flight places. This 'do or die' game was the final game of the four, Sunderland having drawn two and lost one of their previous three 'Test Matches' being the last-placed of the quartet.

The Lads had clearly been dying to get cracking because once the match kicked off at 6.00pm Sunderland tore into Newton Heath and had twice gone close through John Harvie when Gillespie opened the scoring after quarter of an hour. Captain Hugh Wilson began the move finding Hugh Morgan whose cross was headed home by Gillespie.

Morgan went close to getting on the score-sheet himself but it was left to Gillespie to make the game and Sunderland's top flight status safe with his 54th and final goal for the team. A Victorian pitch invasion greeted the final whistle with the ecstatic crowd chairing the victorious players off the pitch.

Gillespie and Campbell were joined by Donald Gow, James Hannah and John Harvie in this being their last game. 'The Team of All The Talents' had established Sunderland as a club of the highest order. Sunderland's pedigree had been proved in the Football

League's formative years. No matter the countless frustrations of future decades, Sunderland fans would always be able to cling to the fact that their club had always been one of the game's elite.

Sunderland weren't a club whose halcyon days surrounded a few cup wins, theirs was a club who had dominated, a club whose team had been the pinnacle of world football – even winning what was considered the 'World Championship' of the time by beating Scottish champions Hearts in an 1895 Challenge Match. The great days of 'The Team of All The Talents' was over. It was time to rebuild but for all their great days: the league titles, the 100 goals in a 30 game season, the finest football of their generation, perhaps this was 'The Team's' greatest achievement. They were past their best, some of their legs had evidently 'gone' but they knew they couldn't let 'Canny Owld Sun'lund' go down and they fought for those stripes when they had to dig into the deepest reserves of their determination at a time when their 'talents' were becoming memories.

Robert Campbell

It would be over sixty years until Sunderland finally succumbed to the second division, some twenty years after no other club could claim to have only ever played in the top flight. That was the legacy of 'The Team of All The Talents' who proved on this day that perhaps the greatest of those talents was sheer guts.

v Bury 3-0

Gigg Lane, Division One
April 16th 1902. Attendance: 10,000

SUNDERLAND	BURY	REFEREE
Doig	Montgomery	Mr. A. Green,
Gibson	Lindsay	West Bromwich
Watson	McEwan	
Ferguson	Johnson	
McAllister	Thorpe	
Jackson	Archer	
Hogg W.	Richards	
Hogg R.	Lamberton	
Millar	Sagar	
Gemmell	Gray	
Murray	Plant	

SUNDERLAND SEALED their fourth league championship with this win. Goalkeeper Ted Doig and forward Jimmy Millar set a club record by each winning their fourth title medal with Sunderland and celebrated in fine style, Doig with a clean sheet and Millar a hat-trick.

Amidst the glory of becoming champions though tragedy lurked. Captain Matthew Ferguson was injured in the game, never played again and was dead less than two months later, passing away from pleuropneumonia at just 29 years of age. A Glaswegian, the first of his 181 games for Sunderland had also been against Bury in 1896. One of two ever presents, alongside Doig, in his first season which culminated in 'The Team of All The Talents' last hurrah in the 1897 Test Match with Newton Heath, half back Ferguson had now led Sunderland as they restored themselves as the country's top club.

In contrast to such a fine servant as Ferguson was William Gibson, the greatest one-game wonder in the club's history. Sunderland had been having a problem at right back. Losing regular full back Andy McCrombie after a comfortable victory over Grimsby the Lads had suffered their worst run of the season going four games

Goalkeeper Ted Doig won his fourth championship medal in this game. Jimmy Millar is the only other Sunderland player to achieve this feat.

without a win as they tried to get over the finishing line. An Irish international when just 17, Gibson had won the Irish Cup the year before with Cliftonville and as an amateur was persuaded by Sunderland to cross the Irish Sea to make what would be the only Football League appearance of his career. (This is a different William Gibson to the one who played in games one and two).

Under manager Alex Mackie Sunderland had been building towards the title. Third in 1900, they had been runners-up in 1901 behind Liverpool who won their first ever championship under the guidance of Tom Watson who had led Sunderland to all three of the Wearsiders' previous triumphs.

Despite the presence of veterans Doig and Millar the 1902 champions were a very different team to Sunderland's previous title winning sides. No previous champions had scored as many as the 100 or 93 goals Sunderland had scored in 1893 or 1892 but none had scored as few as the meagre fifty Sunderland scored in winning the league in 1902 – and in four more games than those earlier champions.

Top scorers Billy Hogg and Jimmy Gemmell scored just ten apiece. Millar's hat trick (his second of the season) brought his tally to nine, ending a league goal drought that stretched back to November, despite the man who is still Sunderland's joint seventh-highest scorer having played regularly throughout the season. Like Peter Reid's

Jimmy Millar

'Division One' winners of 1996 though this side was based on a tight defence. Starting with a 1-0 win at reigning champions Liverpool on Boxing Day, Doig set what in 2010 is still a club record of seven successive clean sheets in league and cup. Helping protect him were stalwarts McCrombie, Sandy McAllister, and left back Jimmy Watson who emigrated to Canada and whose descendants were delighted to witness their only ever soccer match when Sunderland played a friendly in Vancouver in 2005. Players such as those mentioned here may have played before your granddads were born but their legacy lives on.

This was the fourth season at Roker Park and the first time the title had been won since the Newcastle Road years. Following the recent winless run, Millar settled nerves with the opening goal quarter of an hour into the game, turning in a Bobby Hogg cross.

Bury were a decent team who would finish seventh, had beaten Sunderland earlier in the season and would win the FA Cup with what is still a record cup final score-line (6-0) the following season and they made it anything but easy for the Wearsiders. Inevitably the visitors tired, having been forced to play part of the game with only nine men in those pre-substitute days. Archer was injured in a clash with Ferguson (who later returned to the game) while Plant also missed a chunk of the match through injury. Sunderland took full advantage, Millar scoring in the 80th and 90th minutes. His second came when he rolled back the years and dodged past two or three defenders before finishing. Billy Hogg (no relation to Bobby) set up his hat-trick goal seconds before the whistle heralded Sunderland as champions. Millar would follow Ferguson to his grave within five years, the hat-trick hero succumbing to tuberculosis at the age of 37.

v Newcastle Utd 9-1

St. James' Park, Division One
December 5th 1908. Attendance: 56,000

SUNDERLAND	NEWCASTLE UTD	REFEREE
Roose	Lawrence	Mr. A.E. Farrant,
Forster	Whitson	Bristol
Milton	Pudan	
Daykin	Liddell	
Thomson	Veitch	
Low	Willis	
Mordue	Duncan	
Hogg	Higgins	
Brown	Shepherd	
Holley	Wilson	
Bridgett	Gosnell	

DOES IT matter what you read in this chapter? Doesn't the score-line say it all? Newcastle 1 Sunderland 9 (nine). That's not a hammering or a good hiding, it is complete and total annihilation. It's easily the biggest score ever between these old rivals and whenever debate surfaces about the comparative merits of Wear and Tyne it's the trump card. Beat that!

Not only is it the record win between the clubs, it remains the record away win ever in the top flight, equalled only once (by the great Wolves team of the fifties at Cardiff in 1955).

In living memory of older supporters at least Gary Rowell is rightly revered for his 1979 hat-trick in a famous 4-1 win on Tyneside but to get your head around this 1908 result consider that two players scored hat-tricks, another got a brace, there was another goal for Sunderland besides and only the woodwork stopped it being ten!

All of Sunderland's five forwards were capped by England during their careers with George Holley (a Seaham lad like Rowell) scoring more goals for England while on Sunderland's books than any other player and more goals against Newcastle than anyone else while playing for the Wearsiders.

There was little sign of the impending avalanche of goals. A week earlier the north east clubs had been pitted against Nottingham's finest, Newcastle beating Forest 4-0 while Sunderland slumped to a 1-0 home defeat against the Magpies of Notts County. With strong characters such as L.R. Roose, Charlie Thomson, Jackie Mordue and Billy Hogg in the side there was no way Sunderland were going to be beaten by a pair of Magpies in consecutive weekends...one for sorrow two for joy!

What makes the 9-1 even more astonishing was that the record victory was achieved against a Newcastle team enjoying the best spell of their club's entire history. Post-war NUFC history centres on United's trio of FA Cup wins in the early fifties but Newcastle have only won the league four times and two of those had been in the four years prior to this match. Even more amazingly Newcastle were to take the title in the season of their record derby defeat! The Black Cats though have always been top dogs in the north east. At no point in history have Newcastle been able to equal Sunderland's tally of league championships. For the Wearsiders to win 9-1 on their rivals' patch at the apex of Newcastle's history, as United claimed the title for the third time in five years, placed a black border on a black and white seasonal success. The Magpies' strips on the day of the derby defeat illustrated that border as Newcastle played in white shirts edged with black.

Unaware of the red and white whirlwind about to hit them, the Tyneside hordes provided St. James' with its record gate of 56,000 including a sizeable contingent from Wearside who no doubt thought Christmas had come early.

First blood was drawn by Sunderland forward Billy Hogg. Born in 1879, the year Sunderland were founded, he came to the club in 1899, won the 1902 championship and played over 300 games. Having left in 1909 to win three Scottish titles with Rangers, Hogg later returned to Wearside to coach the team from 1927 to '34 before dying in January 1937 with the club he loved the reigning league champions and en route to their first FA Cup triumph. Comic book stuff – even

'Roy of the Rovers' though would have struggled to script Sunderland's slaughter of the Geordies.

It took Hogg just eight minutes to open the scoring. Home left back R. Pudan was to have rings run round him by Jackie Mordue who invited Hogg to net and he duly made no mistake, shooting low past United keeper Lawrence. Newcastle fought back only to find Sunderland's legendary goalkeeper L.R. Roose as imperious as ever and Wearside captain Charlie Thomson as uncompromising as he continued to be throughout his career (later being suspended for a month after the 1913 FA Cup final). Never one to take prisoners, Thomson had welcomed Newcastle's debutant centre forward Albert Shepherd to derby match duels by dumping him heavily on the track surrounding the pitch. Evidently the red and whites were well and truly up for the game and were livid when Newcastle were awarded a penalty on the stroke of half-time for a

George Holley, one of two Sunderland players to claim a hat trick.

hotly contested handball decision. No arguing a century ago? Don't you believe it! Shepherd levelled but all that did was to fire up the visitors even more.

Sunderland scored eight times in half an hour after half-time. Holley began the rout two minutes after the re-start, scoring from distance after receiving from Arthur Bridgett. The woodwork then denied Holley but in the 58th minute the same Mordue–Hogg combination that had opened the scoring repeated the trick, Mordue leaving Pudan in his wake before putting a goal on a plate for Hogg. At 3-1 the dam was broken, Newcastle ran up the white flag, the forerunners of the 'Toon Army' were swept away by a tsunami as Sunderland scored seven goals in the finest fifteen minutes of SAFC history.

Holley overtook Hogg to become the first to claim his hat-trick, scoring in the 62nd and 67th minutes, the latter from a Mordue cross. The fourth-highest scorer in Sunderland's history, Holley scored three or more for the Lads on 11 occasions but surely this was the most satisfying.

Left winger Bridgett had created Holley's first goal and got in on the act himself making it 6-0 in the 69th minute at which point the man marking him, Whitson, went for a holiday and limped off. Sunderland were merciless, even a religious man like Bridgett who duly scored again with a screamer two minutes later. The rampant red and whites tore into the demoralised home side, Mordue getting the goal he deserved in the 73rd minute after again embarrassing Pudan. Having begun the scoring, Billy Hogg completed it with Sunderland's ninth goal in the 77th minute. Nine-one! One more than even Michael Palin's 'Barnestoneworth' supporter from his 'Ripping Yarns' series suffered in his deadpan line '8-1, eight bloody one!' Sunderland left back Thomas Daykin never played for the club again. After this result none of the team needed to!

Legend has it that back at Roker Park, supporters watching the reserves thought that the scoreboard operator was taking the mickey when the score from St. James' kept being changed every few minutes in the second half but it was true. Bob Kyle's Sunderland had put on a performance so great that over a century later the result of Sunderland's clinical finishing is indelibly printed on the minds of Sunderland supporters. It is the score-line from longest ago that Sunderland supporters know and another century from now Wearsiders will still not let Tyneside forget it.

v Aston Villa 0-1

Crystal Palace, FA Cup final
April 19th 1913. Attendance: 120,081

SUNDERLAND	ASTON VILLA	REFEREE
Butler	Hardy	Mr. A. Adams,
Gladwin	Lyons	Nottingham
Ness	Weston	
Cuggy	Barber	
Thomson	Harrop	
Low	Leach	
Mordue	Wallace	
Buchan	Stephenson	
Richardson	Hampton	
Holley	Halse	
Martin	Bache	

THIS WAS Sunderland's first FA Cup final. Winning the cup was the holy grail. The club's fifth league title in 21 years would be sealed seven days later but 29 years after first playing in the cup Sunderland were still waiting to lift it. A huge crowd of over 120,000 watched the game, an English record only surpassed in the first Wembley final a decade later. This game was staged at Crystal Palace but thousands couldn't see and in the one further final held here the gate was restricted to 73,000 – that's a Stadium of Light full less!

Given the vast crowd it is perhaps understandable that nerves should get the better of 21-year-old Walter Tinsley, who refused to play leaving the injured George Holley to play the entire game as little more than a strapped-up passenger. Holley missed the sort of chance he made a career of taking and the thousands of Sunderland supporters who had travelled to the capital – many wearing black cat emblems – journeyed back to the north east wondering what might have been.

Villa's Seaton Delaval-born Clem Stephenson knew the outcome all along. During the game he told Sunderland's Charlie Buchan that he'd dreamt Villa would win with Newcastle-born Tommy Barber

The 1913 final v Aston Villa.

heading the winner. Twelve minutes from time Barber duly headed the only goal of the game from a Wallace corner. Poor Barber had but three years to enjoy his cup winning fame; he died on the Somme in 1916.

Stephenson himself came closest to ending his own dream. He was clean through and looked certain to score when Charlie Gladwin hacked him down to concede a penalty which was the first ever penalty to be missed in the cup final. It was kicked well wide by Southwick-born Charlie Wallace, one of four north easterners in the midlanders' team. Sunderland had only three locals. Stephenson's brother Jim was to play for Sunderland in the 1920s.

Maybe Villa's north east connection added bite to the game, certainly being the cup final the stakes were as high as possible especially between two teams who that year denied each other the 'double', Villa finishing as runners-up to Sunderland in the league but what is certain is that a game considered a great cup final was very stop start with several injuries leading to a reported 17 minutes' injury time in the match. Sunderland though were unable to take advantage, winger Harry Martin going closest to an equaliser with a shot that came back off the inside of the post.

It was a day though when Sunderland wouldn't have scored if they'd played 'til midnight. It simply wasn't their day. Even when Villa's goalkeeper Sam Hardy left the pitch for ten minutes leaving them down to ten men with centre half Jimmy Harrop in goal, the Lads could find no way through despite the second and fourth all time SAFC top scorers (Buchan and the restricted Holley) being in the forward line. Twenty goals had been scored en route to the final but the shooting boots evidently hadn't been packed.

If referee Adams had a tough afternoon given the amount of added time, a good portion of it came as a result of the biggest individual duel of the day, which matched Sunderland centre half Charlie Thomson with Villa centre forward Harry Hampton who had scored twice against Newcastle in the 1905 final. Thomson and Hampton had history. A fortnight earlier they'd been up against each other at Stamford Bridge in an England v Scotland match. On that occasion Sunderland's Holley partnered Hampton in the England forward line with Scotland centre half Thomson marking Hampton who scored the only goal of the game by barging Scotland keeper Brownlie into the back of the net.

Never a shrinking violet, Thomson wasn't about to let lightning strike twice if he could help it although late in the game Hampton did attempt to knock Sunderland keeper Joe Butler over the line. Thomson knocked Hampton out at one point while the Villa man also lashed a kick at the Sunderland captain. Football was a tad rougher back in 1913 than it is now. Back then sending offs were extremely rare, indeed at this point only five players had ever been sent off in league or cup while playing for Sunderland and neither Thomson nor Hampton got an early bath. The FA weren't impressed with their running feud though and suspended both for the first month of the following season while the ref also got a ban.

Thomson's suspension was all Sunderland got out of their first final. The FA Cup wouldn't come to Wearside until Raich Carter carried it home in 1937. Despite this 1912/13 must count as the most successful season in the history of the club who added to their cup final bow by winning the league at Bolton a week later. There was another important appointment before then though… a trip to Villa Park to meet Villa in a league game four days after the cup final! Perhaps regretting his decision to duck out of the cup final Tinsley took Holley's place for the league game, by all accounts played at the top of his game and scored Sunderland's goal in a 1-1 draw. Had he been able to conquer his nerves the previous weekend maybe, just maybe, Sunderland would have done the 'double'.

v Bolton W 3-1

Burnden Park, Division One
April 26th 1913. Attendance: 14,000

SUNDERLAND	BOLTON W	REFEREE
Butler	Edmundson	Mr. W. J. Heath,
Gladwin	Baverstock	Burslem
Ness	Feebury	
Cuggy	Glendinning	
Thomson	Greenhalgh	
Low	Whiteside	
Mordue	Donaldson	
Buchan	Jones	
Richardson	Rowley	
Tinsley	Smith	
Martin	Stokes	

SEVEN DAYS earlier Sunderland played in front of the biggest crowd ever to see them – 120,081, a figure only surpassed in English football at the first ever Wembley final a decade later. There were 106,000 less at Bolton's Burnden Park but whereas Sunderland had lost the cup final at Crystal Palace the previous weekend, wet and windy Lancashire was to be the setting for the Lads clinching the championship for the fifth time, the weather denying the Trotters a 'capital gate' according to the *Sunderland Daily Echo*.

Cup final conquerors Aston Villa were Sunderland's rival for the title and were given a 'hearty round of applause' on the same afternoon as they took to the pitch at St. James. As the biggest two clubs in the country, Sunderland and Villa vied for supremacy and each had had designs on becoming the first team to complete the double of league and cup in the twentieth century. Sunderland's victory in this game at Bolton meant that not only had the Wearsiders won their fifth championship but Sunderland and Villa had denied each other the double that would not be won between Villa's feat of 1897 and Spurs' achievement of 1961 – when Sunderland came closest to derailing Tottenham as detailed elsewhere in *Sunderland's Greatest Games*.

Having been beaten by Villa in the cup final, Sunderland had paid a league visit to Villa Park on the Wednesday night between the final and this league clincher at Bolton. Had Villa beaten Sunderland on their own soil they would have opened up the title race but the Wearsiders had earned a crucial draw at Villa Park meaning that two points at Bolton would wrap up the title.

Bolton were a decent side who would finish eighth and had only lost to a penalty at Roker Park earlier in the season so it was far from a foregone conclusion that after the strenuous week they had had Sunderland would come out on top. Visiting skipper Charlie Thomson won the toss and elected to kick with the wind.

The home side tore into Sunderland from the kick off and had a couple of early efforts on goal but Sunderland took command just ten minutes in when spot kick expert Jackie Mordue converted a penalty awarded when Harry Low was brought down by Jones.

Stung by going behind Wanderers redoubled their efforts, coming closest to an equaliser when Donaldson fired in a drive that

Captain Charlie Thomson, followed by Joe Butler and Charlie Buchan, take to the field at Roker Park during the 1912/13 season.

flew narrowly wide of keeper Joe Butler's far post. Butler had come to Sunderland from Glossop North End early in the campaign, debuting in the seventh game of the season after which the Lads found themselves one place off the foot of the table following a disastrous start. The introduction of the new keeper combined with the arrival of tough full back Charlie Gladwin, who debuted in the next game, coincided with a magnificent upturn in fortunes. Going into this match at Bolton, Sunderland had won 23 and lost only 4 of 29 league games as well as reaching the club's first ever English (FA) Cup final and like true champions the Lads responded to the home side's pressure by soaking it up and hitting them on the break.

Once again Mordue was a thorn in the Trotters' side, the Edmondsly-born winger beating Feebury on the right flank and picking out centre forward James Richardson who coolly picked his spot to double the visitors' advantage.

Showing great character and stamina – no squad rotation or subs then of course – Sunderland effectively had the game, and with it the championship, wrapped up by the 24th minute when Richardson netted again to make it 3-0. Captain Thomson played a key role, bringing the ball out of defence and

Jackie Mordue scored a penalty.

feeding Richardson with a superb pass. There was plenty still to do for Richardson who had to hold off Feebury and Baverstock before tucking the ball beyond Edmundson for his 17th goal in 28 games since signing for Sunderland the previous summer.

Managed by the wonderfully named Will Settle, Bolton pulled a goal back just before half-time when from a quickly taken Whiteside throw in, Butler could only turn a centre onto his crossbar with Jones first to the ball to head home the rebound.

Jones' afternoon was to end early as he was carried off midway during the second half leaving the home team a man short as they strove to get back into the game against a resolute Sunderland defence in which Francis Cuggy, Thomson and Low were outstanding.

Charles Buchan

Indeed it was Sunderland who looked the more likely to add to their score after the break, future England left winger Harry Martin being prominent. It was Richardson though who continued to cause most trouble for the home defence. Duly fired up, he had to be calmed down by the referee after a late fracas with home centre half Greenhalgh. Uncharacteristically Richardson then spurned the chance of a hat-trick when he fluffed a great chance from another Martin delivery in the final minute but the points were secure and with them Sunderland were champions of England once again.

Meanwhile back at St. James' Aston Villa ran out 3-2 winners but it was too little too late, Sunderland had denied the title to the team who themselves had deprived Sunderland of the cup. Only 5,000 turned up to Villa's final match as they beat Sheffield United two days later but they couldn't catch the Lads who extended the final winning margin to four points with a Charlie Buchan winner against Bradford 48 hours after Villa's final fixture.

v Middlesbrough 3-0

Ayresome Park, Division One
May 5th 1928. Attendance: 41,997

SUNDERLAND	MIDDLESBROUGH	REFEREE
McInroy	Mathieson	
Murray	Jarvis	Mr. T.G. Bryan,
England	Smith	Willenhall
Clunas	Miller	
Allan	Ferguson	
Andrews	Peacock	
Robinson	Pease	
Wright	Carr J.	
Halliday	Camsell	
Hargreaves	Bruce	
Death	Williams	

THE RELATIVE merits of matches against Middlesbrough compared to derbies with Newcastle can be measured by the fact that this book includes seven meetings with the Magpies while this is the only encounter with Boro to feature in *Sunderland's Greatest Games*. However this game was without doubt one of the most important Sunderland have ever played.

If you thought the 2008/09 top flight table was tight it was stretched more than a workout video compared to the 1927/28 campaign. Sixteen points (two points for a win) separated champions Everton from the bottom-placed team which thankfully turned out to be Boro rather than Sunderland though a draw would have kept the Teessiders up at Wearside's expense.

Going into this final day of the season game at Ayresome Park Sunderland were second bottom, ahead of Manchester United, with Boro and Sheffield Wednesday just above. All four were locked on 37 points with Spurs on 38 but having completed their fixtures. Another six clubs were on 39 points although they could rest easy because only two went down and with Boro and Sunderland locking horns only one could overtake them.

As modern day fans can vouch, Sunderland specialise in making supporters sweat. With five games to go they were 12th (out of 22 remember) but conspired to lose 5-1, 3-1 and then 2-1 to bottom-of-the-pile Man Utd. No matter, a nice last home game to struggling Sheffield Wednesday should make the Lads safe. Evidently the players thought so as they switched off at 2-0 up and contrived to lose 3-2.

Confidence was on the floor, manager Bob Kyle had resigned in March having been in charge since 1905 and injuries weren't helping. Bobby Gurney wasn't fit to play and goalkeeper Albert McInroy was heavily strapped up and sent out to play in place of Paddy Bell who had deputised against Wednesday and took the blame for the defeat.

McInroy proved to be the pivotal figure. Sunderland have a tradition of great goalkeepers and Albert the Great's performance this day ranks right up there with the best you can think of: Monty at Huddersfield '62, Monty at Wembley, Turner at Spurs in '85 or Norman at Wembley in 1990 springing to mind. McInroy's moment came exactly 45 years to the day before Monty's in the 1973 FA Cup final and like Monty that day against Cherry and Lorimer, McInroy's heroics featured a marvellous double save. Without film record we have to go on contemporary reports but by all accounts McInroy's double stop was every bit as good as even Monty's as he flung himself to push a Jacky Carr effort onto the post and then spin back to somehow block Bobby Bruce's follow-up.

In fact despite the score-line Boro battered Sunderland but couldn't beat McInroy. The only goalkeeper to win a full cap for England while on Sunderland's books, he was a fine custodian and later won an FA Cup winner's medal with Newcastle in 1932. Quoted in 'Sunderland's Number Ones' supporter Alexander Kemp, who watched Sunderland from 1924 onwards, remarked: "I've seen many good goalkeepers at Sunderland but none to beat Albert McInroy."

On a blisteringly hot day Sunderland struggled to get out of their half but stunned the home side with a goal in their first attack in the 13th minute thanks to the man most able to cope with the heat,

David Wright, who owned a bakery business. No prizes for thinking he used his loaf!

Undaunted, Boro, who with 81 league goals to their credit had good reason to think they'd score and get at least the draw they needed, kept attacking. At centre forward they boasted George Camsell. He'd set a league record with 59 goals the season before as they were promoted and had over 30 to his name in the higher division. It wasn't Camsell's day. As he saw McInroy stop everything he hit at him, over at Goodison Park Dixie Dean was netting a hat-trick for Everton against Arsenal to reach 60 goals for the season and remove Camsell from the record books just as Sunderland were removing Boro from division one.

Albert McInroy, the only goalkeeper to play for England while on Sunderland's books.

Sunderland's own goalscorer supreme was Dave Halliday and ten minutes after half-time he struck to double Sunderland's advantage. Five minutes later it was all over as Wright set up the appropriately named Billy Death to make it 3-0 and condemn Boro to the drop. Sunderland had performed heroically. Centre half Adam Allan had arguably his finest game for the Lads while full backs Ernie England and Bill Murray were immense.

Murray had arrived from Cowdenbeath a year earlier in a double deal with Wright and would become one of the longest-serving players in SAFC history, being with the club until 1957 as player and then manager with just a two year stint back in Scotland breaking that spell. Three decades after the game Murray told the great north east football historian Arthur Appleton: "There was the drama of strong men weeping [in the dressing room afterwards]. The atmosphere was unreal."

Astonishingly in the dressing room that day Murray was paired with a man who had been at the club since 1897, the pair of them linking the club's early years with the living memory of older modern day supporters. In charge of Murray and his teammates that day was Billy Williams. Since his arrival at the club before Sunderland even moved to Roker Park, he had been the trainer and the man much more responsible for the running of the team than manager Kyle. Taking charge of the side in the closing stages of the season he felt the weight of protecting Sunderland's unbroken run in the top flight. "It was the only time I saw old Billy crying" McInroy informed Appleton.

Williams would stay at Roker for one more year, helping the new manager settle in. That new manager watched Sunderland from the stand that day at Ayresome Park. He was Johnny Cochrane who would steer the club to league and cup triumphs in the thirties. That decade of Carter and co is considered one of SAFC's most glorious but the 20s is the forgotten decade. It is the only one since the club entered the Football League in 1890 that hasn't seen a league title, cup final, promotion or relegation. Even the war-torn forties saw a war-time cup final but Sunderland had been a decent side in the twenties. In the five years prior to this Boro showdown they'd been runners-up twice, third twice and seventh. They had nothing to show for their efforts but like the 'Team of All The Talents' in the 1890s they summoned up one last great effort to save the club from relegation and themselves from ignominy.

v Arsenal 5-4

Roker Park, Division One
December 28th 1935. Attendance: 58,773

SUNDERLAND	ARSENAL	REFEREE
Thorpe	Moss	Mr. H.E. Hull,
Morrison	Male	Stockport
Hall	Hapgood	
Thomson	Crayston	
Clark	Roberts	
McNab	Copping	
Davis	Rodgers	
Carter	Bowden	
Gurney	Drake	
Gallacher	Bastin	
Connor	Beasley	

THE 1973 cup classic with Manchester City was voted the best match in Roker Park's 99 year history when the ground closed in 1997 but *Sunderland's Greatest Games* claims that this game was better. True, the City game was fantastic but there weren't too many people around in 1997 who had seen this game more than six decades earlier to vote for it and consider the facts.

Arsenal had been league champions for each of the last three seasons and in four of the last five. Sunderland had been runners-up the year before and had set Arsenal's never to be surpassed record Highbury crowd during that campaign.

When Wearside welcomed Arsenal between Christmas and the New Year Sunderland were top of the table and boasted a magnificent home record of played ten, won ten with no fewer than 40 goals scored in those ten triumphs. Bobby Gurney had scored five in one game earlier in the month and, looking to depose Arsenal as champions, Sunderland couldn't wait to rip into the Londoners at Roker and did so. Sunderland led 4-1 at half-time only for the Gunners to show the qualities that had brought them a hat-trick of titles by fighting back in the second half leaving Sunderland to edge

The Sunderland team of the mid-thirties.

a nine goal thriller that featured some of the top stars of the 1930s, a time when people suffering from the Depression needed football to lift them from the gloom. Perhaps fittingly, fog had threatened the match on the morning but there were still close to 60,000 expectant souls assembled as what was to be an immense game kicked off.

Seven minutes in, Sunderland took the lead when right winger Bert Davis drove Sandy McNab's left wing cross home after centre forward Bobby Gurney's dummy fooled the champions' defence. With Ted Drake prominent, the Gunners pressed for an equaliser but just ten minutes after opening the scoring, Davis turned provider, setting up Patsy Gallacher to head home.

Arsenal halved the deficit mid-way through the half from the penalty spot, the legendary Cliff Bastin scoring after he was brought down by Jimmy Clark. Conceding goals didn't bother Sunderland! They would go on to win the league that season despite letting in more goals – 74 – than any other side in the top half of the table. Sunderland simply scored for fun, a club record 109 league goals in the season being 28 more than anyone else in the top half of the league managed. In 2002/03 Sunderland didn't even score 28 goals in total (21 in fact).

Raich Carter and Bobby Gurney each scored over 30 league goals during the season and it was Carter, skipper in the absence of Alex Hastings, who scored in the 35th and 44th minutes to give Sunderland a big half-time lead. Carter's first was a low shot under the keeper while his second came from the penalty spot after he'd been barged over by Herbie Roberts.

Imagine Arsenal manager George Allison's half-time team talk. Presumably it was along the lines of 'go out there and show why the league title hasn't left Highbury since 1932' and the visitors came out determined to play like the champions they were. Sunderland's centre forward Gurney may well have scored five in a match earlier in the month but it was only a fortnight since Arsenal's Drake had netted no less than seven in a match and before five minutes of the second half had elapsed he'd made it 4-2. Sunderland's Sandy McNab got the final touch but Drake's shot was on its way in anyway and when Ray Bowden reduced the arrears further when heading home a Roberts cross Sunderland could have buckled. However there were two sets of champions on the Roker pitch that day, the outgoing and the incoming and Sunderland simply did what they did all season – just made sure no matter how many they let in more were scored at the other end.

For many supporters left winger Jimmy Connor was their favourite. Gallacher having picked up an injury, he was switched to the flank (no subs in 30s league games) with Connor taking over at inside left and it was from there that Connor scored the goal that proved to be the winner. Taking possession on the halfway line he raced forward leaving a couple of defenders in his wake as he traded passes with Carter before firing home from outside the box at the Fulwell End.

Goalkeeper Jimmy Thorpe, sadly to pass away the following February.

To Arsenal's credit they fought to the last, making it 5-4 with quarter of an hour still to play when Bowden got his second of the game with the help of a deflection off Clark who had thus given away a penalty and deflected a shot into his own net and yet could make a claim to be man of the match for the manner in which he shackled Drake, one of the most dangerous forwards of the age. In the spirit of the age Sunderland simply kept attacking, looking for another goal rather than shutting up shop but the scoring was over and Sunderland ran out 5-4 winners in a game where football itself was the winner.

A Sunderland forward line of a year earlier. Left to right: Jimmy Connor, Patsy Gallacher, Bobby Gurney, Benny Yorston, Bert Davis. Yorston had left by the time of the Arsenal game, Raich Carter joining the rest of this forward line for the nine goal thriller.

Having been top of the table for two months Johnny Cochrane's side never relinquished top spot as they became champions of England for the sixth time. Sunderland have never won the title since and yet even now only five clubs have won it more times. Sadly goalkeeper Jimmy Thorpe never received his championship medal. It was given to his widow instead, diabetic Thorpe dying less than six weeks later after receiving rough treatment in a game with Chelsea.

v Birmingham 7-2

St. Andrew's, Division One
April 13th 1936. Attendance: 21,693

SUNDERLAND	BIRMINGHAM	REFEREE
Mapson	Clack	Mr. C. Booth,
Morrison	Barkas	Heywood
Hall	Steele	
Thomson	Stoker	
Johnston	Sykes	
McNab	Loughran	
Davis	Jennings	
Hornby	Devine	
Gurney	Clarke	
Carter	Harris	
Connor	Morris	

A S REFEREE Mr. Booth of Heywood sounded the final whistle Sunderland were confirmed as champions of England for the sixth time. It was a feat only Aston Villa could equal although the Villans hadn't been champions since 1910 and, come the end of the season, slipped out of the top division along with Blackburn Rovers, leaving champions Sunderland as the only club in the country who could proudly proclaim that the only league they had ever played in was the top one.

The Wearsiders could hang on to the boast of being the only club to have never played outside of the top flight for a further two decades but the fact that there are now two clubs (Manchester United and Liverpool) with three times as many titles as Sunderland – for whom 1936 remains their last – is a sad indictment on the club's post war record.

However at St. Andrew's on Easter Monday 1936 Sunderland produced a performance to cap a season any champions at any time in the game's history would be proud of. Runners-up the year before, Sunderland had ended Arsenal's run of three consecutive titles with three games to spare. The title was sealed in sensational style, seven

Sunderland's all time top scorer Bobby Gurney who scored four times as the title was sealed at Birmingham.

goals being stuck past Birmingham despite their keeper Frank Clack having the proverbial 'blinder' and former Sunderland player Joe Devine playing out of his skin. Sunderland apparently played like Arsenal do now with the emphasis being more on scoring beautifully crafted goals rather than simply a lot of them. Mind you with 109 in the league by the end of the season Sunderland netted 20 more than the second highest scorers. This was the second time during the season Sunderland had won 7-2. On the earlier occasion (v Bolton Wanderers in December) Bobby Gurney had scored five, on this occasion the man who is the club's all time record scorer hit four.

Two years before he passed away in 1994 Bobby told me: "We beat them 7-2. I scored four of the goals and I probably could have scored another two or three. The forward line was: Davis, Carter, myself, Hornby who played instead of Gallacher and Jimmy Connor was on the left wing. To a certain extent it was a wonderful game of football from a Sunderland point of view. It was very one sided, but it gave us players great satisfaction because we clinched the league. We stayed in the New Street Station that night celebrating. We lost games after that but we knew nobody could catch us."

Two days earlier Sunderland had lost 2-1 at Bolton but they weren't about to let another opportunity of being crowned champions pass them by. In the days when clubs traditionally played three games in four days over Easter, Sunderland had beaten Birmingham 2-1 at Roker Park on Good Friday thanks to two goals from the now injured Patsy Gallacher.

April showers of bursts of heavy rain and even hail and snow were interspersed with brief spells of sunshine but Sunderland had proved themselves a team for all seasons. They made light of the conditions producing football of the highest order with Raich Carter on top of his game. Skippering the side in the absence of Alex Hastings who had picked up a knock at Bolton, Carter chose a special occasion to demonstrate that he was arguably the finest footballer ever to pull on a Sunderland shirt.

Gurney made the most of playing in front of one of the game's greatest ever inside forwards and settled any nerves Sunderland might have had by giving the Lads the lead in the 14th minute when he latched onto Carter's defence-splitting pass to rifle past Clack. It was Clack though who kept his side in the game, twice spectacularly denying Gurney before Birmingham drew level in the 31st minute when Joe Loughran beat Sunderland's teenage goalkeeper Johnny Mapson.

Mapson was making only his fourth appearance. Regular goalkeeper Jimmy Thorpe had lost his life two months earlier dying in a diabetic coma five days after playing in a rough match with Chelsea at Roker Park. Matt Middleton had kept goal for nine games but lost his place when a run of five games without a win for the top-of-the-table team culminated in a 6-0 hammering at Middlesbrough.

Mapson's debut coincided with a return to form and he would go on to become a great goalkeeper but at this stage Sunderland's greats were largely in the forward line. Mapson was beaten again four minutes before half-time through Albert Clarke who equalised for a second time, Carter having put Sunderland ahead in the 36th minute thus registering Sunderland's 100th league goal of the season when powerfully shooting past Clack after receiving from Jimmy Connor.

Not as famous to the modern day supporter as Carter, Gurney or Mapson, Connor was nonetheless the favourite of many supporters at the time. The great Sunderland historian Billy Simmons always insisted to me that the mercurial Connor was the best player he'd ever seen play for Sunderland. Connor was the architect behind the visitors regaining the lead two minutes after the home side had made it 2-2, Connor providing the cross for Cyril Hornby to head his first goal for the club.

Though Sunderland went in ahead at the interval it was by the odd goal in five from a game they had dominated. They were to be ruthless in the second half though. After going close several times in the first few minutes Sunderland made it 4-2 in the 55th minute through Gurney who rolled the ball over the line after dribbling around Clack. Some originally gave the goal to Carter who applied a finishing touch but only after the ball had already entered the goal.

Eight minutes later Gurney completed his hat-trick with a superb shot from the edge of the box after being fed by Carter. There was no let up as Sunderland attacked relentlessly, Gurney making it 6-2 with his fourth of the game when he headed home Bert Davis' 75th-minute corner before Connor completed the scoring four minutes from time, capitalising on Carter's third 'assist' of the game.

v Preston North End 3-1

Wembley, FA Cup final
May 1st 1937. Attendance 93,495

SUNDERLAND	PRESTON N.E.	REFEREE
Mapson	Burns	Mr. R.G. Rudd,
Gorman	Gallimore	(London)
Hall	Beattie	
Thomson	Shankly	
Johnston	Tremmelling	
McNab	Milne	
Duns	Dougal	
Carter	Beresford	
Gurney	F. O'Donnell	
Gallacher	Fagan	
Burbanks	H. O'Donnell	

"THAT'S A nice wedding present for you," said the Queen as she handed the FA Cup to Sunderland skipper Raich Carter. Carter had married Rose Marsh on the Monday before the cup final with centre forward Bobby Gurney as his best man. Carter and Gurney had scored 31 goals each the previous season as Sunderland claimed their sixth league championship but the town yearned for the glamour of a first cup win.

A panoramic view of the 1937 cup final.

The faces of the cup team.

It was Sunderland's first ever game at Wembley which opened ten years after the Lads' solitary previous final when defeat had cost them the 'double'. The Roker Park club had finished eighth in the league, six places and three points better off than Preston with each side beating the other in their home league fixture but it was North End who many considered favourites. The Lilywhites had thumped West Brom in the semi, Spurs 3-1 at White Hart Lane in the quarter-final, scored five in both the 5th and 4th rounds and knocked out Newcastle in the third round – not a bad little cup run. In contrast Sunderland had just edged out the first ever third division semi-finalists (Millwall), needed two replays to win a quarter final with Wolves and had only beaten lower league opposition in the earlier rounds.

Moreover PNE centre forward Frank O'Donnell had scored ten goals en route to Wembley including two hat-tricks and a brace in the semi. North End captain Tremmelling won the toss and his side were quickly on top. Faster to the ball, Preston enjoyed the better of the first half and when they took the lead seven minutes before half-time

61

through Frank O'Donnell he became only the third player ever to score in every round. The goal came from a free kick conceded by Jimmy Gorman. The kick was partially cleared but Dougal and Hugh O'Donnell, the scorer's brother, worked the ball back to the in-form striker who got past Sunderland centre half Bert Johnston to beat Sunderland 'keeper Johnny Mapson.

Mapson was spending his last day as a teenager playing at Wembley. It would be Peter Shilton in 1969 who broke his record as the youngest FA Cup final goalkeeper. He had no chance with the goal and was almost pressed into serious action again moments later when Sunderland had a serious let-off. "We could have gone two down," Mapson recalled in the book *Sunderland's Number Ones*: "O'Donnell – who'd scored the first goal – came through the middle again and Bert Johnston, who was playing centre half, turned round and chased him. I came out to the edge of the penalty area and just before he was ready to part with the ball Bert caught him and took him down – or it could have been two. He'd have been sent off these days and it was a let off. If we'd been two down we might have been in trouble, but second half there was only one team in it."

Captain Carter spoke up at half-time, recalling in his autobiography that he'd stressed: "It is more important we score our own goals. We have got to be more in the game. We have got to make the ball work more, find the man more. Don't be nervous. Let's play football as we can play it, and we will be alright."

Attack was always the best policy for Sunderland's brilliant side of the thirties. When the title was won a year earlier the Lads had let in more goals than anyone in the top 12 – but had scored 20 more than anyone else. In the cup year even the relegated teams had conceded less than Sunderland but the forward line could devastate any opposition, as Preston, whose line-up included future Liverpool legend Bill Shankly, were about to find out.

Six minutes into the second half centre forward Gurney headed the equaliser after Carter knocked on Eddie Burbanks' corner. This was at the same end where Ian Porterfield would score the winner in the '73 cup final after Dave Watson knocked on Billy Hughes' corner. Providers Carter and Burbanks would add their own names to the score-sheet before the afternoon was over. Preston pleaded the goal was offside but Beattie had played Gurney on.

Roared on by the tens of thousands who had travelled from the north east, Sunderland were rampant. Uncharacteristically Carter missed a great opportunity: "I had a chance of putting us ahead, but muffed the shot.... I topped it and to my dismay it went not into the goal but into the side of the net. A moan went round the stadium but that was nothing to my own feelings. I was the unhappiest man on the field. I had had my chance and lost it."

It was only a matter of time until Sunderland went ahead. Given the let-off they'd enjoyed late in the first half there could be no grumbles when the referee played on when gifted inside left Patsy Gallacher was felled in the box.

North End were hanging on the ropes until Sunderland delivered a 'one-two' knockout blow. On 71 minutes Carter scored a captain's goal meeting a bouncing cross from Gurney – living up to his role as Carter's best man: "I beat the full back and goalkeeper to the ball and lobbed it out of his reach. We both went down together but I saw that the ball had reached the net." Seven minutes later left winger Burbanks received from his inside left Gallacher and gave former Newcastle keeper Mickey Burns no chance. The cup was on its way to Sunderland.

Action from the final.

Raich Carter

It was the first time an FA Cup final had been televised and also the first time the cup had been presented by the Queen. Given Sunderland's previously miserable luck in the competition the club hadn't organised any post-match event so some of the players went to Preston's reception instead although no one could blame Raich Carter for departing to see his bride.

For Preston, manager Tommy Muirhead resigned afterwards, but their day would come a year later when they won the final, a last-minute penalty beating Huddersfield keeper Bob Hesford whose son Iain would keep goal for Sunderland four decades later.

Having triumphed at Wembley Sunderland took the train back from King's Cross to Newcastle. On Tyneside they were met by the Mayor of Newcastle, a band and afforded a civic welcome. From there it was on to Wearside where as Raich Carter recalled: "...was like stepping on to an alarm signal. Suddenly everything went off. The tugs and ships in the river were hooting and blowing their sirens, railway engines shrilled their whistles, bells rang and rattles clacked, there was shouting and cheering. It was a thick, concrete wall of deafening din. Then the cheering resolved itself into a Sunderland roar: 'Ha'way the Lads!' And the cry was taken up and surged round, echoing and re-echoing through the crowd who spread further than the eye could see. 'Ha'way, ha'way, ha'way!' cried half a million throats."

The cup winners of 1937.

Sunderland had won the cup at last and in a town where the first thing keeper Johnny Mapson noticed when he signed a year earlier was that the children in the street wore no shoes as the north east was hit hard by the depression, as has been the case so often the people of Sunderland find heart, expression and pride in the football team that unites everyone who lives in 'the Sunder'd land'.

v Huddersfield T 6-2

Roker Park, West Riding (Combined
Counties) Cup final, first leg
May 1st 1943 Attendance: 8,000

SUNDERLAND	HUDDERSFIELD T	REFEREE
Clark	Curnow	Mr. K. Evans,
Gorman	Bailey	Darrington,
Eves	Mountford	Yorkshire
Housam	Willingham	
Lockie	Brown	
Hastings	Boot	
Spuhler	Thompson	
Laidman	Barclay	
Whitelum	Price	
Carter	Baird	
Lloyd	Watson	

FOUR SUNDERLAND players have scored five times in a match:
Jimmy Millar against Fairfield in the record 11-1 win of 1895, the
club's highest ever scorers Charlie Buchan and Bobby Gurney both
achieved the feat on December 7th, Buchan against Liverpool in 1912
and Gurney 23 years later against Bolton. Since the war only one
man has done it: Nick Sharkey against Norwich in 1963. During the
war itself though Cliff Whitelum scored six goals in one match – and
he chose a cup final to hit his double hat-trick in.

Wartime football was complicated although in the circumstances
there were more things to care about than the intricacies of football
competitions – people were just pleased to have a game to attend to
take their minds off things for a couple of hours or so.

Rather like they do now in Argentina for example wartime
football employed an 'opening' and a 'closing' championship.
Sunderland managed to finish 22nd in the 'opening' table which
took into account games up to Christmas Day despite winning more
games than they lost out of the 18 played. In the second half or
'closing' championship the Lads rose to the dizzy heights of 20th,
nestled in between Aberaman Athletic and Rochdale.

Bomb damage at Roker Park.

Suffice to say Sunderland were not involved in the 'finals' tournament and instead decided to participate in the West Riding (Combined Counties) Cup. This involved two-legged ties starting with Middlesbrough, a 1-0 second leg away defeat not creating much of a stir as Boro had been walloped 8-0 in the first leg at Roker. The second round or quarter-final paired Sunderland with Bradford City where the second leg did matter as after losing the first game 5-2 in Yorkshire, Sunderland won on aggregate after a 5-1 home victory. City's rivals Bradford Park Avenue – for whom Len Shackleton played during the war – were then beaten 1-0 away before a 2-2 home draw secured a place in the final with Huddersfield.

Sunderland had been in a cup final a year earlier losing the League War Cup final over two legs to Wolves. In that final Sunderland only managed a home draw in the first leg but with home advantage again in the first game against Huddersfield a big lead was quickly established.

Cliff Whitelum was 23 at the time. He'd made his debut as a teenager before the war in a 1-1 draw at Blackpool and had been given one more game, an end-of-season goalless stalemate at Wolves. During the war he served six years with the Royal Artillery and became a prolific scorer in the wartime game totalling 130 goals in 167 matches, all but 41 of those appearances being for Sunderland.

This was his finest day. Everything he touched seemed to find the back of the net. Providing the ammunition was schemer supreme, Raich Carter. He of course had captained Sunderland in winning the FA Cup exactly six years ago to the day. Here before a crowd of 8,000 in the middle of the war, that glorious day beneath the twin towers must have seemed a lifetime away. Carter had spent the first two years of hostilities as a member of the auxiliary fire service but in October 1941 had enlisted in the R.A.F. After training at Blackpool he was posted to a fighter operational training unit near Sunderland as a physical training instructor, hence his availability to play. Carter had turned out occasionally for Huddersfield as a 'guest' during the first

Cliff Whitelum astonishingly scored all six of Sunderland's goals.

year of the war and gave the Terriers the run-around at Roker.

Star of the show of course was Whitelum who scored five goals without reply in the first half. He'd previously scored four in the earlier rounds and had a dream 45 minutes where everything he hit flew past Huddersfield goalkeeper Curnow. With Carter, Alex Hastings and Johnny Spuhler all on top form the chances just kept coming and Whitelum took full advantage. He added his and the team's sixth to extend the lead after half-time.

In later years Whitelum would achieve the creditable record of 20 goals in a total of 50 Sunderland appearances, scoring twice in each of the first two post-war league games – the second of them against Huddersfield. His only peace time hat-trick – just the single not the double this time – was a noteworthy one, coming in a 3-0 win away to Manchester United played at Man City's Maine Road as Old Trafford was bomb damaged. Roker Park hadn't emerged unscathed, twice being bombed including just two weeks after Whitelum's six-goal feat – a bomb going through the roof of the main stand.

Despite his more than decent record Whitelum was sold for Sheffield United's record fee of £9,000 in October '47, some of that money no doubt going to fund the purchase of Shackleton from Newcastle four months later. At Bramall Lane Whitelum would score 15 goals in 41 appearances before moving into the non-league game. It is his misfortune that war-time games and goals do not count in official records but nonetheless as the only man to score six goals in a game for Sunderland – and in a cup final at that – he should not be forgotten.

What Sunderland did forget was that even at 6-0 a game isn't won until the final whistle – especially if there is a second leg to play before the match is over. Having sat back thinking the cup was won, Sunderland allowed the visitors to twice reduce the deficit on Wearside. Both goals were scored by Billy Price. He'd joined Huddersfield from an outfit called Wrockwardine Wood Juniors from the Wellington area in 1937, had scored on his debut against Derby in 1938 and twice scored 40 goals in a season during the war.

Huddersfield were no mugs and included 12-times capped England right half Ken Willingham who during the war was a fitter and turner in munitions works. Nonetheless their supporters decided there wasn't much chance of them overturning a four-goal first-leg deficit as only 2,626 attended the second leg.

Each side made two changes for the return leg a week later, Sunderland were without Carter and Arthur Housam, replacing them with Bradwell and Robinson while Huddersfield switched Malpass and Rickett in place of Thompson and Reg Mountford who was an ARP. A Watson hat-trick added to a goal by new man Rickett would have tied things for the home side but for what proved to be the decisive goal from Johnny Spuhler.

It's never a bad thing to win a trophy and although the 1943 West Riding (Combined Counties) Cup was hardly going to cause dancing in the streets, for Cliff Whitelum the tie gave him a unique place amongst Sunderland goalscorers.

v Manchester Utd 5-3

Old Trafford, Division One
Boxing Day 1950. Attendance: 37,024

SUNDERLAND	MANCHESTER UTD	REFEREE
Mapson	Allen	Mr. R.A. Mortimer,
Hedley	Carey	Huddersfield
Hudgell	McGlen	
McLain	Gibson	
Walsh	Chilton	
Wright A.	Cockburn	
Bingham	Bogan	
Wright T.	McShane	
Davis	Aston	
Broadis	Pearson	
Watson	Rowley	

THIS WAS typical of the 'Bank of England team' of the fifties. They'd missed out on the league title the previous season through slipping up at home to relegation doomed Manchester City late on. In this campaign they'd finish a disappointing 12th and yet could turn out results like this one away to a side destined to be runners-up. The previous away game had been lost 6-5 at Derby, the fifth successive away reverse, indeed there had only been a solitary away win thus far. However since that 11 goal game at Derby – the fourth and last time 11 goals had been scored in a Sunderland match – there had been creditable home wins over Liverpool and Manchester United, both in the previous three days.

Two goals from 'Rock on' Tommy Wright had beaten United on Christmas Day. The day though was to belong to a man who just under two years earlier had transferred himself to Sunderland when player-manager of Carlisle: Ivor Broadis.

Really called Ivan but universally known as Ivor, Broadis was just 23 when appointed player-manager of Carlisle – who he was still watching as a reporter when well into his eighties in 2010. "Players didn't have many rights in those days," he explained: "There was the maximum wage and effectively players were soccer slaves…I wanted to go to Sunderland where they treated their players very well and did all they could for them. When we travelled or stayed at hotels for instance, everything was first class."

Broadis was undoubtedly first class himself at Old Trafford where he scored a hat-trick as Sunderland completed a third successive away win over United. Anyone missing the first few minutes after they'd tucked into their Boxing Day dinner would have missed the opening two goals. The pitch was slippy and both defences conceded before they began to get used to it.

Just two minutes had gone when the home side took the lead through John Aston, an England international whose son of the same name would be part of the United team who became the first English side to win the European Cup 18 years later. Sunderland hit back straight away, home keeper Reg Allen misjudging the bounce of a Dickie Davis cross on the hard surface and leaving the young Northern Irish winger Billy Bingham to accept the Christmas Box of an easy tap in for his first goal in English football. Bingham would go

Dickie Davis had been the country's top scorer the previous season and is seen in action here at Roker Park.

on to become a huge figure in the game; playing for and managing his country in the World Cup finals.

From then on Sunderland dominated but they had to wait almost half an hour to take the lead. When it came though it was with another burst of two goals in as many minutes but this time both were for the Wearsiders who wrested control of the match.

Davis had a hand in both goals, his 29th-minute shot coming back off the bar to Broadis who instantly netted the rebound. As United reeled, Broadis took possession again within a minute of the restart and burst through the home defence. Seeing Davis unmarked he tried to play him in only for the pass to be intercepted and roll back invitingly into his own path. Once again Broadis was no sooner going to look a gift horse in the mouth as he'd snapped up his own transfer to Sunderland and he tucked his shot past Allen to make it 3-1.

After their domination Sunderland probably felt the score-line reflected their performance. If any eyes were taken off the ball as the half-time refreshments were wondered about, United made them pay by pulling a goal back. This time Aston was the creator, tricking Arthur Hudgell and Bill Walsh before crossing for Tommy Bogan who forced home a close-range effort.

Sunderland manager Bill Murray may well have been planning an angry half-time team talk as his side didn't have a game they were dominating already wrapped up, but two minutes before the break the two goal cushion was restored when Broadis completed his 14-minute hat-trick to make it 4-2. "The ground was bone hard but the team played very well that day," remembers Ivor. "It was one of my best games for Sunderland."

A stylish inside forward who would later be capped 14 times by England, Broadis was as much a creator as a scorer of goals. He duly made Sunderland's fifth goal just past the hour mark with a nifty back-heel indicative of a player bursting with confidence. Davis was the beneficiary having been the chief first half goal maker. A schoolboy international teammate of Shackleton, Davis had been the first division's top scorer the previous season but was often used as an inside man following the record signing of Trevor Ford. However Ford missed the Christmas double header allowing Davis to lead the line.

Ivor Broadis

At 5-2, Sunderland cruised home to make it a very happy Christmas despite United scoring a consolation through Bogan's second of the game four minutes from time, Glaswegian Bogan netting a rebound when Johnny Mapson in the Sunderland goal couldn't hold a Pearson shot. Sunderland's FA Cup winning keeper from 1937, Mapson had played alongside United manager Matt Busby for Reading during the war – they'd won the 1941 Wartime Cup as teammates and Busby had attempted to sign Mapson for Manchester. With eight goals on a hard pitch it may not have been a day for goalkeepers but it was certainly one of the highspots in the Sunderland career of Ivor Broadis.

v Arsenal 7-1

Roker Park, Division One
September 12th 1953. Attendance: 59,784

SUNDERLAND	ARSENAL	REFEREE
Cowan	Swindin	Mr. H. Webb,
Hedley	Barnes	Leeds
Hudgell	Evans	
Anderson	Forbes	
Daniel	Dodgin	
Snell	Mercer	
Bingham	Logie	
Wright T.	Lishman	
Ford	Milton	
Shackleton	Holton	
Elliott	Roper	

SUNDERLAND AND Arsenal's stature as dual powerhouses of English football was brought to the fore in the 1930s. In this eighth post-war league campaign the Gunners arrived on Wearside as reigning champions. However they were enduring something of a hangover as they were still without a win in this their eighth game of the season. Sunderland weren't doing much better having won just one of their half-dozen fixtures and losing their previous home game 5-4. Nonetheless the house full signs were up at Roker with just under 60,000 hoping to see Sunderland's 'Bank of England' team cash in.

England international Billy Elliott had been one of Sunderland's big signings in the summer. Injured at Charlton on the opening day, he was making his home debut beginning an association with SAFC that would see him play over 200 games, become trainer to the 1973 FA Cup winners and have two spells as caretaker manager, the latter for over half a season when he took the team to within a whisker of promotion in 1979. Loyalty in football was common at this time, Arsenal manager Tom Whittaker – London born but Tyneside raised – had been with the Gunners since 1919. Sadly he would pass away of a heart attack just three years later. Someone who had moved was

Len Shackleton in action against Arsenal.

wing half Ray Daniel; he'd only missed one game as Arsenal won the league the year before but he too had come to Sunderland for a big fee during the close season and would have a fine match.

When Sunderland met Arsenal during this era there was always the added attraction as you paid your money at the gate of knowing that the brightest star in Sunderland's parade of big names would be guaranteed to be 'up' for the game. Len Shackleton had been rejected by Arsenal as a youngster and made no secret of the fact that he always wanted to show them what they'd missed. At Highbury he once sat on the ball before shooting to illustrate how much time he'd made himself after waltzing through their defence: "You'll never make the grade as a footballer," former Arsenal manager George Allison had told him. Shack himself said: "I have been given the title of Arsenal's star attraction just because I seem to reserve all my best displays for Sunderland games against the club who sacked me," although he denied he had anything to prove.

In the first half there was little sign of Shack putting on a show as Sunderland struggled. For all their star names Sunderland were more often a set of individuals rather than a team. Arsenal took the lead and with better finishing that lead could have been unassailable. Their great inside forward Doug Lishman eventually found the back of the net in the 26th minute having earlier wasted two presentable chances while Cliff Holton had missed a sitter as early as the eighth minute. The crowd weren't impressed as Sunderland were outplayed by their winless opponents but an equaliser out of the blue seven minutes before half-time completely changed the complexion of the game.

The biggest single problem with Sunderland at this time was the clash in personality and style of Shackleton and centre forward Trevor Ford, the legendary Wales striker. Ford was a 100 per center who scored a lot of goals and grafted for every one of them. Shack was as talented as any player in the game – Stanley Matthews said Shack scored the best goal he ever saw in international football, and against the reigning world champions at that – but could frustrate as well as he could delight because he had to be 'in the mood'. Shackleton and Ford notoriously wouldn't pass to each other or Shack, who could weigh a pass to within half an ounce, would apparently sometimes deliberately overhit a ball aimed at Ford. Today though Sunderland were playing Arsenal and Shack laid the ball on for Ford to finish.

After playing well but being pegged back, the visitors' fragile confidence ebbed, Sunderland seizing advantage to somehow manage to go into the break ahead, debutant Elliott slamming home a powerful drive after terrific combination play from Stan Anderson, Billy Bingham and Ford who had all now clicked into gear.

Sunderland didn't want the half-time whistle to come but they continued as they left off with Shack now concentrating more on the prince rather than the clown aspect of his moniker. He got the third himself in the 68th minute, Ford making it 4-1 straight away as Arsenal collapsed, conceding five goals in the game's final quarter. The hard-working Tommy Wright was in the middle of a seven match run where he netted in every game and he wasn't slow in bagging a couple against dispirited opponents in the 78th and 81st minutes, the latter from an Elliott corner.

The only member of the five man forward line not to score was right winger Billy Bingham but he capped a fine individual

Billy Elliott made a scoring home debut.

performance by crossing for Ford to complete his hat-trick two minutes from time. Sadly Ford would play just six more games before being only too glad to leave. Calling Sunderland "the graveyard of centre forwards" and saying of Shack; "what a pity his clowning has been allowed to nullify much of the co-ordination of the forward line" adding, "Shack and I were as different as chalk and cheese…there never seemed any chance of us hitting it off as part of a team."

If a team win 7-1 these days you are likely to hear the chant: "Can we play you every week?" Had Sunderland been able to play Arsenal every week when Shack was around maybe 'The Bank of England' team might have been worth the money paid for them.

16 v **Newcastle Utd 2-0**

St. James' Park, FA Cup 6th round
March 3rd 1956. Attendance: 61,474

SUNDERLAND	NEWCASTLE UTD	REFEREE
Fraser	Simpson	Mr. R.H. Mann,
Hedley	Batty	Worcester
McDonald	McMichael	
Anderson	Stokoe	
Daniel	Paterson	
Aitken	Scoular	
Bingham	Milburn	
Fleming	Davies	
Holden	Keeble	
Elliott	Curry	
Shackleton	Mitchell	

IN THE 1999 derby that resulted in Ruud Gullit getting the sack the Magpies blamed the rain, on this occasion it was apparently the wind to blame at least if you believe Tynesiders. Certainly the wind was strong enough to make the match lack quality football and in all honesty not merit inclusion in 'Greatest Games' but when it comes to greatest results it was right up there. A 2-0 win while welcome may not be the stuff of legend even in a derby game but consider the following: The Magpies had enjoyed their greatest ever derby win on Boxing Day, humiliating the red and whites 6-1 at Roker Park before rubbing it in with a 3-1 home victory 24 hours later, plus the Magpies were looking to retain the FA Cup for the second time in the fifties having won it in '51, '52 and '55. Thirdly and most importantly having divested Newcastle United of silverware in 1956, going into the 2010/2011 season the Tynesiders were still seeking their next major domestic trophy!

In a game featuring the big names of Sunderland's 'Bank of England' team and the cup heroes of Tyneside it was Bill Holden who made this game his own, scoring both goals. His only previous goal for Sunderland had come on his debut at St. James' and he

The queue for 1956 cup quarter-final tickets at Roker Park.

would score only four more for the club before seeing out his career with Stockport, Bury and Halifax. He was the toast of the 16,000 Sunderland supporters in the all-ticket gate of 61,474 that gave the Geordies their record receipts of £9,600, admission prices having increased for the first cup meeting between the north east giants since before World War One.

Norwich, York and Sheffield United had been Sunderland's victims so far in the cup run whilst the Magpies had seen off Sheffield Wednesday, Fulham and Stoke. Sunderland had needed replays to see off two of their three cup scalps but Newcastle had won each tie at the first time of asking and, given their handsome double over the Wearsiders earlier in the season combined with home advantage, they were ready to top up their order of silver polish believing that once again the cup would be coming to St. James'.

Bob Stokoe had won a cup winners' medal with the Magpies less than a year earlier and would of course lead Sunderland to the cup as manager seventeen years later when his trainer would be Billy Elliott who gave Stokoe a tough time at St. James' with a 'man of the match' display.

Sunderland's away form was inconsistent to put it kindly. The 'Bank of England' side evidently could beat the best when they turned it on but more often than not they would not combine as well as they were capable and therefore often came a cropper. Early in the season they'd let in seven at Blackpool and since shipping eight at Luton in November they'd lost five out of six away trips in the league including a 3-0 reverse at West Brom in the game before the cup quarter-final. Typically of the 'Shack' era the only away game they'd won during this spell was at the home of reigning champions Chelsea while in the cup they'd managed goalless draws at third division York and Sheffield United, destined to finish bottom of division one that season.

Both teams wore away kits as was the norm in the fifties if there was a colour clash in the cup and it was the away team who adapted better to the conditions with Charlie 'Cannonball' Fleming, Elliott and Len Shackleton giving the home defence problems. Shack had scored six goals on his Newcastle debut in 1946 but had no time for the Tynesiders, famously remarking: "I'm not biased when it comes to Newcastle, I'm not bothered who beats them."

Stan Anderson was already in his fourth season and would stay at Sunderland until 1963 before a controversial move to Newcastle.

Len Shackleton

It was Shack who created the opening goal four minutes before half-time, finding Holden who netted with a back header to leave 45,000 Geordies listening to the Roker Roar welcoming the goal.

Duly boosted, the visitors dominated the second period and eventually got the second goal their performance merited when United defender Bill Paterson had a 'David Corner moment' and lost the ball when he could have put it out. Holden was the man who picked his pocket and made the game safe. Holden's first goal was an instinctive header befitting a man who attended the same school as Tommy Lawton but this was a fine individual strike. Having pressurised Paterson to dispossess him, Holden displayed the kind of composure not normally associated with derby games to cut in and coolly pick his spot.

Newcastle's glorious cup era of the fifties would see them fail to get past the fourth round for the rest of the decade, being knocked out by Millwall and Scunthorpe along the way. They'd enjoyed a tremendous spell but Sunderland had brought it to a shuddering stop.

v Tottenham H 1-1

Roker Park, FA Cup quarter-final
March 4th 1961. Attendance 61,326

SUNDERLAND	TOTTENHAM H	REFEREE
Wakeham	Brown	Mr. A. Murdoch,
Nelson	Baker	Sheffield
Ashurst	Henry	
Anderson	Blanchflower	
Hurley	Norman	
McNab	MacKay	
Hooper	White	
Fogarty	Allen	
Lawther	Jones	
McPheat	Smith	
Dillon	Dyson	

TWO GREAT FA Cup quarter-final games were played at Roker Park in 1961 and '64, both on March 4th, but the Sunderland line up for this game with Spurs and three years later against Manchester United had only two players who featured in both games (Ashurst and Hurley) as manager Alan Brown built a team to take Sunderland back to the top flight, the club having lost its treasured position as the only club never to have played at any level other than the top level following a first ever relegation three years earlier.

Rotherham, Brighton and Bristol Rovers were the next names on the fixture list so the visit of Bill Nicholson's 'Push & Run' Spurs was a huge attraction for Sunderland who were finally on the up after a dreadful period. Having finished in the bottom half of the second division in their first two years in it, the Lads were fifth off top when Spurs came north in the knowledge that Arsenal had been beaten at Roker in the third round, Sunderland having followed that up with solid away wins at fellow second division promotion-seekers Liverpool and Norwich. Spurs though had won all but one of their last eight away games and were en route to becoming the first team in the twentieth century to achieve the 'double' of league and cup. That

Sunderland came so close to preventing this is stated in Spurs' own official illustrated history where Sunderland's goal is described as: "Perhaps the single most worrying moment during the 'double' season."

It hadn't looked like the Lads would cause their illustrious visitors much of a problem as Spurs dominated, looking well in control having gone ahead as early as the ninth minute when Cliff Jones headed home from 12 yards at a Roker End corner. Tottenham's ability to swiftly move the ball around left Sunderland chasing even more shadows than they did in training under Alan Brown's famous 'shadow play' and to all intents Spurs were cruising, Les Allen threatening a second, Jones forcing Colin Nelson to clear off the line, Smith hitting the post and powerful Dave Mackay causing havoc with a succession of enormous throws into the box.

Sunderland had a lot of tough characters in their side though, people like Len Ashurst, Jim McNab, Charlie Hurley and Stan Anderson for instance were never going to roll over. Sunderland had won their last five home games and champions elect or not, Spurs weren't going to leave Sunderland without a fight. Sunderland might have been second best before half-time but they still managed to threaten an equaliser, Hurley threatened at set pieces, Anderson brought a good save out of Bill Brown and little John Dillon on the left wing had probably his best game for the club, proving a real handful as he took on Tottenham, at one point in the second half even impudently 'nut-megging' the imperious Spurs skipper Danny Blanchflower.

The Roker Roar really cranked up in the second half as Sunderland had a right go. Dillon won a 50th-minute corner and from it Sunderland drew level. The scorer was Willie McPheat, an 18-year-old Scottish centre forward who had impressed enough to be brought back into the team after injury even though his replacement in the previous game (John Goodchild) had scored a hat-trick at Leeds. The biggest moment of McPheat's career arrived when as so often happened Sunderland scored after Hurley thumped in a header from a corner. Hurley had been the first centre half in the game to go forward for corners and time after time a goal came from the tactic. On this occasion the Irishman's header was parried by Brown and in the melee, McPheat was first to the rebound to make it one each.

"I was only about two yards out, the goalkeeper palmed the ball out to me and I was in the right place at the right time and that was that, everything went loose!" Willie remembered.

Roker Park erupted but supporters overcome with emotion poured onto the pitch to celebrate the equaliser. Having got Spurs on the canvas though this allowed them to take a few breaths rather than being subjected to Sunderland coming at them again. The wily Blanchflower picked the ball up out of the back of the net and told the ref: "Let the fans work it off, we don't mind."

"It was a disadvantage that the fans came onto the pitch because it gave Danny Blanchflower a chance to get Tottenham organised but you can't blame the supporters, they were just excited," McPheat recalled. "I was excited as anyone and everyone was going bananas! The crowd was absolutely fantastic that night."

Blanchflower was a player of style and panache but even he was forced to resort to fouling as Spurs struggled for survival. He brought Ian Lawther down for a free kick that Len Ashurst delivered to cause more consternation leading to three corners in a row as Sunderland piled on the pressure. Dillon, Harry Hooper and Amby Fogarty all tested Brown, Dillon coming closest with a 75th-minute effort that Brown saved with the assistance of a partial block that took some of the weight off the shot.

Although they were penned back for much of the time Spurs had their chances too, John White seeing a diving header clear the bar and Terry Dyson bringing a good save out of Peter Wakeham.

At the final whistle Sunderland could take satisfaction from the fact they had given the best team in the country – probably the best team in England over three or four decades – the toughest game of their greatest season. Wearside had left an indelible imprint on Blanchflower who after the game was found wandering the empty stands looking for loudspeakers he thought must have been used to amplify the crowd. He hadn't experienced technology; he'd heard the Roker Roar.

"I remember playing at St. James' Park in 1952 … I remember sitting with a capacity crowd in Barcelona as Barcelona beat their arch rivals Real Madrid, but nothing I have ever heard equalled the intensity of that wild roar at Roker Park," said Blanchflower of one of Sunderland's greatest games.

Spurs would turn on the style and win the replay 5-0 but north east supporters were proud of their team as Len Ashurst remembers: "Alighting from the train on our return to Sunderland the following evening we discovered hundreds of supporters thronging the railway station wanting to express their appreciation for a great cup run."

Willie McPheat equalises and the crowd invade the pitch giving Spurs time to recover.

18 v Norwich City 7-1

Roker Park, Division Two
March 20th 1963. Attendance: 42,393

SUNDERLAND	NORWICH CITY	REFEREE
Montgomery	Kennon	Mr. A. Holland,
Nelson	Kelly	Barnsley
Ashurst	Staton	
Anderson	Scott	
Hurley	Ashman	
McNab	Mullet	
Davison	Mannion	
Herd	Bryceland	
Sharkey	Allcock	
Crossan	Hill	
Mulhall	Punton	

"**W**HEN KEVIN PHILLIPS** was playing for Sunderland I used to worry every time he scored four goals in a game. I always want Sunderland to win and win well, but I quite like being the only man alive who can claim to have scored five goals in a game for the club." The words of Nick Sharkey who was still a teenager on this Wednesday night in 1963 when Sunderland ran riot against a Norwich side previously unbeaten in an eight game run where they'd conceded only five times and scored 26 themselves.

A prolific scorer as a youth team player, Sharkey had once scored an incredible 13 goals in one game. Following the 'big freeze' in 1963 Sunderland had only played four league games since Brian

Nick Sharkey

Clough had been badly injured on Boxing Day at a time when he had scored 28 goals in as many games. Young Sharkey had been brought in to replace the legendary goal machine but was yet to find the back of the net in league games since coming into the side. He had shown his potential in cup games though scoring four goals in four games, including one against Aston Villa in the first leg of Sunderland's first ever League Cup semi-final.

The top of the table was tight. Sunderland were second but just two points ahead of fourth-placed Stoke who had two games in hand with fast-rising Norwich just two points behind them. Only two places were up for grabs and it was still two points for a win.

Sunderland won the game handsomely and deserved to. They had to work for it, the Canaries offering stiff resistance until Sharkey broke the deadlock in the 35th minute but in fact Sunderland could have had it so much easier. In his hard hitting autobiography *Left Back in Time* Sunderland left back Len Ashurst, a man who later managed Sunderland and also holds the club record for most outfield appearances, tells of a Norwich approach to fix the match. "One of the Norwich City players approached Charlie Hurley and I in the players' corridor. They had heard we were to receive this huge bonus if we took the two points and this particular player was suggesting to Chas that a number of the Norwich City team would be prepared to throw the game for some remuneration. Not for the first time Charlie ...refused to accept to bend."

Sunderland may well have made the match more difficult for themselves by declining the offer from the visiting player but once young Sharkey opened the scoring, finishing off a slick move involving Johnny Crossan and George Herd it was all one way traffic. Sharkey would complete his hat-trick before the interval, benefitting from the approach work of Jim McNab and George Mulhall.

Sunderland hit Norwich with a second burst of three goals in nine minutes, this time all of them from corners. Opposing sides simply couldn't handle the presence of Charlie Hurley at set pieces and Sunderland often profited. In the 57th minute Stan Anderson made it 4-0 with a powerful header from Mulhall's flag kick. On the hour Sharkey snapped up his fourth of the game with a diving header after Hurley had won Jimmy Davison's corner. Sunderland were piling on the pressure against wilting opponents. Three further corner were won in the next few minutes and from the last of them Johnny Crossan got on the score-sheet to add to the hat-trick he'd scored in the previous game.

At 6-0 Sunderland cruised home, Norwich gaining a tiny consolation five minutes from time when Irish international Jimmy Hill (not the ex Fulham player and *Match of the Day* presenter) finished off a pass from ex Wolves winger Gerry Mannion.

Nick Sharkey at home with the ball he scored five goals with.

Within a minute Sunderland restored their six-goal lead when Sharkey wrote himself into the record book as only the fourth man ever – and the only one post-war – to score five goals in a competitive peacetime game for the club. It was a typical poacher's goal, the teenager still sniffing out the chance for a goal four minutes from time when he'd already scored four. His enthusiasm meant he was first to the ball when keeper Sandy Kennon could only push a Mulhall shot onto the post.

Sharkey had got the headlines but it was a tremendous team performance: "the finest all round display from a Sunderland team for many years" according to the *Sunderland Echo*. While the youngster enjoyed reading the following day's papers and carried home the match ball, his older team mates had something extra to celebrate.

Len Ashurst in his study.

Nick explains: "After a performance like that you'd expect the senior players to be delighted for you [but] they seemed to be even more pleased than I might have expected. I didn't know at the time but the senior players were on a bonus based on their league position at certain points in the season and this was one of them. Len Ashurst and I still joke about it because the senior players got around £1,000 after that result and all I got was the ball! The bonus wasn't in my contract. We won the game 7-1 and I was happy getting the ball at the time. Through the years, though, the ball is worth more to me than the money, so it's a joke now, but was serious at the time!"

v Everton 3-1

Roker Park, FA Cup 5th round
February 15th 1964. Attendance: 62,851

SUNDERLAND	EVERTON	REFEREE
Montgomery	West	Mr. A. W. Luty,
Irwin	Brown	Leeds
Ashurst	Meagan	
Harvey	Harris	
Hurley	Labone	
McNab	Kay	
Usher	Scott	
Herd	Stevens	
Sharkey	Gabriel	
Crossan	Vernon	
Mulhall	Temple	

S O OFTEN overlooked when people consider Sunderland's great-est games due to the epic three game quarter-final with Manchester United and the glorious first ever promotion-winning game against Charlton all in the same season, this fifth round tie saw second division Sunderland not only beat the reigning league champions but do so with a scintillating performance in front of a gate just short of 63,000.

Sunderland's battles with Leeds in the sixties and seventies climaxed in the 1973 FA Cup final and included a fierce three game cup clash in '67. In 1963/64 the bitter rivals were promoted together, Leeds taking the title but Sunderland taking three points out of four off them. Sunderland players of that era are adamant to a man that they were the better side and the Everton game helps to support that view. Everton had knocked Leeds out in a fourth round replay at Goodison and it hardly bears thinking about what might have happened if Sunderland and Leeds had gone head to head in the cup in '64 as they were neck and neck in the promotion race. Indeed it was only in the week of the three quarter-final games that Leeds sneaked ahead of the Lads who went up as runners-up.

The queue for tickets for the cup tie with league champions Everton.

Champions Everton were in fine form when they came to Roker. Seven days earlier they'd enjoyed a handsome 3-1 win over Liverpool and their last away game had brought a comfortable 3-0 victory at a Sheffield Wednesday side good enough to finish sixth in the top flight that year. Everton themselves would finish third having won the Charity Shield and only going out of the European Cup at the hands of Internazionale of Milan who went on to win it and retain it the following season.

In the mood Charlie Hurley and co were in they wouldn't have minded taking on Inter, never mind Everton. The last six home games had been won, six had been scored in each of the last two and rivals Leeds were amongst the half dozen to go home with their tails between their legs. The attitude was 'Champions? Bring them on.' The side was the classic line-up of this fabulous season, from Monty to Mulhall unchanged for the 12th game in a row.

In the white heat of the Roker Roar, Everton succumbed in just three minutes. From a corner won by right winger Brian Usher, his opposite winger George Mulhall returned a long ball into the box where 'Mac the Knife' applied the killer blow: left half Jimmy McNab giving keeper Gordon West no chance. Sunderland had scored 25 goals in their previous seven games and felt they could score every time they went forward. They were especially potent at corners but even with England centre half Brian Labone and future England keeper West the Toffees failed to heed the lesson.

"Whenever we got a corner in those days Charlie Hurley used to stride up from the back and defences could get quite panicky about having him around the box," says nippy striker Nick Sharkey while Hurley himself muses: "I was pretty good in the air and I caused havoc! The idea of a centre half moving forward was brand new …centre halves never went up for corners or free kicks until then but afterwards it became an absolute must…whenever we got a corner or a free kick near the box the chant would go up right around the ground, 'Charlie! Charlie!' and in those days crowds didn't really chant or sing in the way they do now."

Everton knew full well what Sunderland would do but they were powerless to prevent it. Sure enough Mulhall took another corner, Hurley powered onto it at the back post to score with Sharkey following up just in case. Quarter of an hour gone, 2-0: welcome to Wearside.

Sunderland were rampant. Remember this was a second division side playing the league champions and this was in an age when FA Cup games were the biggest games of anyone's season. Within another five minutes Sunderland had scored a third. Sharkey was the provider, feeding the mercurial Scottish international inside forward George Herd. Herd's cross found the back of the net courtesy of a deflection from defender Mick Meagan.

Stung by conceding three goals for the first time since the turn of the year, Everton came forward and reduced the deficit before half-time, Brian Harris scoring with a powerful header from Alex Scott's free kick after the winger had been upended by ex Liverpool man Len Ashurst who always liked to familiarise his winger with the cinder track that surrounded the pitch.

With defenders of Hurley and Ashurst's calibre not to mention the superb young Montgomery in goal, Sunderland could defend when they had to and though the Toffees tried all they could think of after the break-in the end they resorted to long balls which were meat and drink to Hurley.

The boys of '64 in training. Left to right: Cec Irwin, Jimmy Montgomery, Martin Harvey, Nick Sharkey (mainly hidden), Charlie Hurley, Len Ashurst, Jimmy McNab.

Everton would go on to win six and draw two of their next eight first division fixtures but had been well beaten at Roker Park. Sunderland would go on to a sensational cup epic with cup holders Manchester United and to win promotion. The Everton game was one of the highlights of a great season and given the result and quality of the opposition arguably the greatest performance of that celebrated campaign.

v Manchester Utd 2-2

Roker Park, FA Cup quarter-final replay
March 4th 1964. Attendance: 46,727
(unofficially estimated 70,000-80,000)

SUNDERLAND	MANCHESTER UTD	REFEREE
Montgomery	Gaskell	Mr. E. Crawford,
Irwin	Brennan	Doncaster
Ashurst	Dunne	
Harvey	Crerand	
Hurley	Foulkes	
Elliott	Setters	
Usher	Herd	
Herd	Chisnall	
Sharkey	Charlton	
Crossan	Law	
Mulhall	Best	

HAVING KNOCKED out league champions Everton in the fifth round, Sunderland's reward was a quarter-final away to cup holders Manchester United. With 86 minutes gone at Old Trafford Sunderland deservedly led 3-1 only for an injury to keeper Jim Montgomery to let United back into the game. Cup fever hit Wearside big style. Three years earlier to the day Roker Park had witnessed one of its greatest games at the same stage of the cup against Tottenham and no one wanted to miss out on another cup classic.

It is commonly believed that the north east's biggest ever official attendance was surpassed on this evening. 75,118 had witnessed an FA Cup clash at Roker with Derby 31 years earlier almost to the day and while officially the attendance was just 46,727, the gates at the Roker End were forced 45 minutes before the scheduled 7.30 kick-off and barbed wire was cut at the Fulwell End. Thousands poured in, many more who arrived at the ground gave up and went home as there was not a space to be had with the crowd up over the normal perimeter fence. It is estimated that between 70 and 80,000 squeezed into Roker Park leaving the players a bit miffed that they didn't cash

The Sunderland team listen to the FA Cup draw that gave them a quarter-final away to cup holders Manchester United.

in on their crowd bonus of a fiver a man for every 1,000 supporters on the gate once 55,000 was passed. Of more importance was that two of those supporters didn't make it home as they died at the match. Given the crush and the forced gates it is perhaps fortunate that even worse didn't occur.

Those that did see the game, saw a top class cup tie with Sunderland once again more than a match for a United side including Bobby Charlton, George Best and Denis Law, all of whom would become European Footballer of the Year between 1964 and 1968. The visitors began positively but it was Sunderland who were the first to show when George Mulhall found Johnny Crossan. The pair had scored Sunderland's three goals at Old Trafford between them and would torture United once again, this time though Crossan's shot cleared the bar as Sunderland attacked the Fulwell End.

Hurley then went close with a trademark header from a Brian Usher corner that just cleared the bar and as the Lads confidently took the game to the visitors, Martin Harvey was next to threaten after receiving from Cec Irwin only for his shot also to be too high. Sunderland's marauding young full backs Irwin and Ashurst were getting forward at every opportunity and it was from another Irwin cross that Mulhall headed just over. David Gaskell wasn't being tested in the United goal but Sunderland's onslaught had the vast crowd right behind them. Sharkey and Crossan had further efforts on goal before United displayed their attacking prowess as Bobby Charlton crossed for the 17-year-old Best but Monty had read it and spectacularly intercepted the cross. Charlton then combined with Law who supplied Phil Chisnall who wasted what was a good chance.

With three minutes to go to half-time it had been typically frenetic cup fare with plenty of excitement but neither keeper had been tested. What was needed was a moment of inspiration and there were plenty of players on the pitch capable of providing that. One of them was Nick Sharkey. "I'll always remember one against Manchester United. I even have a photograph of it in my front room – a perfect overhead kick," recalls Sunderland's centre forward. It certainly was a great goal, Sharkey positioning himself perfectly to scissor kick a perfect volley from the edge of the box as he capitalised on a weak clearing header from a throw in. Not everyone in the packed ground had a good view of it but those who'd clambered onto the roof of the Clock Stand had the view but not the balance and in the celebrations that followed more than one had to hang on to their mate for fear of plunging onto the crowd below.

Sunderland were good second half starters and often scored soon after the restart. They piled into United upon the resumption, Hurley

Game 1: *James 'Blood' Hannah.*

Game 4: *James Gillespie was the two goal hero.*

Game 4: *The Newcastle Road ground on the occasion of its final league game almost exactly a year after the Newton Heath 'Test Match'.*

Game 6: *How St. James' Park looked at the time, although this picture is from Sunderland's return there in the FA Cup later in the same season as the 9-1 win.*

Game 7: *A souvenir of the cup final.*

Game 7: *1913 cup final ticket.*

Game 7: Charlie Buchan.

Game 7: *Jimmy Richardson scored twice.*

Game 12: *Bobby Gurney heads the equaliser.*

Game 11: *Legendary winger Jimmy Connor.*

Game 12: *Parading the cup back on Wearside.*

Game 12: *"That's a nice wedding present for you," says the Queen as she hands the cup to Raich Carter.*

Game 14: *Tommy Wright in 2009 with an article about him in the Sunderland match programme.*

Game 15: *Billy Elliott at home in his 80s.*

Game 17: *Cec Irwin, John Dillon and Willie McPheat discuss the Spurs game.*

Game 17: *A ticket for the game, note in 1961 it's still referred to as the English Cup.*

Game 20:
Len Ashurst and Denis Law.

Game 18: *Left to right: Stan Anderson, Jimmy Montgomery and Len Ashurst in 2010. Only Victorian keeper Ted Doig can join them in Sunderland's all time four leading appearance makers.*

Game 21: *The 1964 team reunited. Back row left to right: Johnny Watters (physio), Colin Nelson, Cec Irwin, Charlie Hurley, Jimmy Montgomery, Stan Anderson, Jim McNab, Len Ashurst. Front row left to right: Brian Usher, George Herd, Nick Sharkey, Johnny Crossan, George Mulhall.*

Game 23: *Vic Halom scores his legendary goal.*

Game 24: *Vic Halom gives Sunderland the lead.*

Game 25: *Reliving old times. Left to right: Dave Watson, Dick Malone, Jimmy Montgomery and Ron Guthrie.*

Game 25: *Bob Stokoe embraces Monty at the final whistle.*

Game 25: *Bobby Kerr lifts the cup.*

Game 25: *Ian Porterfield with the Golden Boot given to the scorer of the winning goal in the cup final. Here with full backs Dick Malone and Ron Guthrie.*

Game 25: *Monty makes his brilliant save.*

Game 25: *Ian Porterfield's goal.*

Game 25: *The cup reunion. Left to right: Dennis Tueart, Billy Hughes (hidden), Jimmy Montgomery, Mick Horswill, Dave Watson (hidden), Bobby Kerr, Ron Guthrie, journalist Bob Cass, Dick Malone, Ritchie Pitt, David Young, Vic Halom.*

Game 25: *Jimmy Montgomery with the cup he did so much to win. The cup reunion. Left to right: Dennis Tueart, Billy Hughes, Jim Montgomery, Mick Horswill, Bobby Kerr, Dave Watson (hidden), Ron Guthrie and journalist Bob Cass.*

Game 26: *Dennis Tueart scores from the spot against Vasas in the home leg.*

Game 26: *Vic Halom.*

Game 30: *Tony Towers receives the Second Division trophy from Newcastle and Football League chairman Lord Westwood as Sunderland chairman Keith Collings looks on.*

Game 31: *One of Gary Rowell's goals from his 1979 hat-trick at Newcastle.*

Game 34: *Clive Walker looks back on his hat-trick as the highlight of his time at Sunderland.*

Game 32: *Stan Cummins in action.*

Game 38: *Marco in action in the home leg.*

Game 38: *Gary Owers is still
Sunderland through and through.*

Game 39: *Paul Hardyman.*

Game 39: *Marco Gabbiadini, Gary Bennett, Peter Davenport
and Paul Bracewell celebrate.*

Game 40: *Gordon Armstrong.*

Game 41: *Gary Owers tackles Dean Saunders as Anton Rogan, Kevin Ball and Brian Atkinson close in.*

Game 41: *Anton Rogan and Gary Bennett squeeze out Ray Houghton.*

Game 41: *Michael Thomas gives Liverpool the lead.*

Game 42: *Lionel Perez.*

Game 43: *Niall Quinn celebrates.*

Kevin Ball lifts the trophy at the end of the 1998/99 season.

Kevin Phillips relives old times in 2010.

Chris Makin and Nick Summerbee in 2010 with Jimmy Montgomery.

Game 45: *Niall Quinn celebrates his goal.*

Game 1:
Niall and Superkev both scored.

Game 46:
Phillips scores his second and Sunderland's third goal.

Game 47:
Emerson Thome and a young Julio Arca.

SUNDERLAND'S GREATEST GAMES

Chairman Niall Quinn.

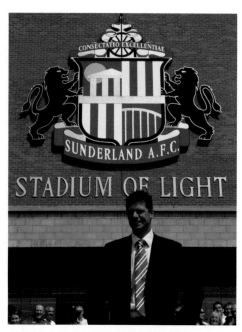

Game 50: *Darren Bent scores the quickest goal of the Premier League season, after just 36 seconds against Spurs, April 2010.*

and Mulhall threatening before Sunderland appeals for a penalty for handball were waved away. The second goal just wouldn't come though and on the hour Manchester threatened through Best and Law. Sunderland's defence held firm but United claimed a fortunate equaliser in the 62nd minute when Montgomery's goal kick went straight to Law who took full advantage by closing in to score.

An exciting game saw both sides have further chances with Sunderland still on top but the Lads couldn't find the back of the net again until 40 seconds into extra time. Receiving from Harvey, Sharkey hit a searching ball destined for George Herd who would have had a sitter but only for Maurice Setters to turn the ball into his own net. Sunderland now led in the tie yet again. They'd never been behind in the three hours thus played but could tired limbs hang on for another half an hour? There was a let-off when Law hit the bar but luck was to desert them two minutes from full time when Bobby Charlton headed the equaliser from a David Herd centre.

In those far off days of second replays the sides would reconvene at Huddersfield five days later in between Sunderland league games with Middlesbrough and Newcastle from which weary Sunderland took a solitary point having failed to score. Sharkey did score again against Manchester United to give Sunderland the lead in the second replay. "We were six inches deep in mud," recollects Sharkey. "I did the wrong thing again, I scored the first goal. That really got United's gander up, so they lashed us 5-1. Manchester United were a great team and when they finished us off, they finished us off right and proper. Having said that, in two of the three games we should have beaten them."

v Charlton Athletic 2-1

Roker Park, Division Two
April 18th 1964. Attendance: 50,827

SUNDERLAND	CHARLTON ATH	REFEREE
Montgomery	Wakeham	Mr. W. Crossley,
Irwin	Hewie	Lancaster
Ashurst	Kinsey	
Harvey	Bailey	
Hurley	Tocknell	
McNab	Edwards	
Usher	Matthews	
Herd	Peacock	
Sharkey	Kenning	
Crossan	Firmani	
Mulhall	Glover	

A S WITH so many of Sunderland's greatest games, this one was about pure emotion. In Sunderland, people don't simply support a team in the manner many around the country think normal. On Wearside and throughout County Durham Sunderland supporters eat, sleep and breathe SAFC. Weddings, Christenings, holidays, you name it, it gets organised around the fixture list. No topics of daily conversation are more common than how Sunderland played last time out, what the manager should do and a consideration of the Lads' chances in their next match.

With that in mind consider the blow suffered in 1958 when for the first time ever Sunderland were relegated. For two decades they had been the only club to be able to boast that they'd only ever played in the top flight. It had been a long road back. The previous two seasons had seen Sunderland finish third when only two were promoted and there were no play-offs. The second of these near misses had been especially hard to take as a last day home defeat to rivals Chelsea had cost promotion when only a draw had been needed.

Only one league game had been lost since Christmas but no one was counting any chickens when fourth-placed Charlton came to

Roker. The visitors had no chance of promotion but were a decent side free from pressure who could prove to be party poopers. Sunderland were virtually up before kick-off. They'd need to lose both remaining games and third-placed Preston win both of theirs to stand a chance of being thwarted and even then Preston would need to improve on a massively inferior goal average...but after the near misses already endured nothing was being taken for granted.

Anxiety amplified when Charlton took the lead in the 17th minute through Eddie Firmani. Preston were away to lowly Bury and news filtering through from Gigg Lane was that North End were ahead. In goal for Charlton was former Sunderland man Peter Wakeham. He'd produced some good performances for Sunderland before losing his place to Jim Montgomery but was playing like a man possessed on his return.

This though was to be Sunderland's day, the footballing gods offering a bit of help with the equaliser two minutes before half-time. The inspired Wakeham was left with no chance when George Herd's shot struck Charlton defender Brian Tocknell and spooned over Wakeham, dropping into the net for an own goal. A bit more good fortune came the Lads' way straight after the resumption when visiting defender John Hewie was injured. Two seasons later

The Lads on the lap of honour.

King Charlie takes the salute.

Charlton's Keith Peacock became league football's first ever substitute but here Charlton had to limp on with ten and a half men with Hewie at first going off, and being severely restricted when coming back on. Nerves had got the better of Sunderland though as the team who had played with such verve all season felt the weight of expectation.

Wakeham continued to play what was commonly considered to be 'the game of his life'. Indeed Monty would have been proud of saves he made to thwart Hurley, Sharkey and Herd. With a minute to go Sunderland got the goal they craved. Top scorer Johnny Crossan killed a Mulhall cross stone dead and blasted it beyond Wakeham.

Cue pandemonium. Sunderland were back in the big time. As it turned out Bury had fought back to beat Preston so Sunderland would have been guaranteed promotion even if they'd lost to Charlton and there was still one more game to play at doomed Grimsby anyway.

Captain Charlie Hurley was named as runner up to West Ham's cup-winning captain Bobby Moore as Footballer of the Year, the nearest any Sunderland player has been to claiming the award. It was a day 'King' Charlie will never forget: "Even now when I meet Sunderland supporters they talk about that day," says Charlie, now well into his 70s. "We did a lap of honour and went back to the dressing rooms, but we could still hear this unbelievable noise from outside. The chairman, Syd Collings, came in and said: 'You'll have to go out again lads.' We were all half dressed and about to go in the bath but we went out again. The roars of 'Charlie! Charlie!' were fantastic and so the team lifted me onto their shoulders – no mean feat – and chaired me around the pitch. It will always go down as the greatest day of my footballing career, and I played from when I was 17 until I was 35 so that says it all."

In 2010 in Sunderland, the *Football Echo* is an institution of over 100 years' standing and one of the nation's last four Saturday evening football papers to survive. In 1958, in shock at Sunderland's first ever relegation, it turned from pink (which it had been since 1937 when Sunderland won the FA Cup for the first time) to white and then a horrible pasty blue for the six years in the second division wilderness. When ecstatic supporters got their hands on the 'Footy Echo' that night they found that like everyone in the town the paper was 'in the pink'.

v Portsmouth 3-2

Fratton Park, Division Two
December 9th 1972. Attendance: 5,841

SUNDERLAND	PORTSMOUTH	REFEREE
Montgomery	Horn	Mr. R. Tinkler,
Malone	Hand	Boston
Coleman	Collins	
McGiven	Wilson	
Watson	Stephenson	
Porterfield	Munks	
Kerr	Piper	
Horswill	Reynolds	
Hughes	Hiron	
Chambers	McCann (Lewis)	
Tueart (Tones)	Jennings	

THE FINAL three minutes of this match were arguably as important a 180 seconds as any in the entire history of Sunderland AFC. It was Bob Stokoe's first away match after becoming manager and within five months Sunderland went from 19th in the second division to glorious FA Cup winners with a league placing that these days would qualify for a play-off place to boot. But for the last three minutes of this largely forgotten fixture on the south coast, history may have been very different.

Sunderland had lost Stokoe's first match in charge but given it was at home to table topping Burnley by just 1-0, and that Stokoe had

Bobby Kerr

Billy Hughes

endeared himself to the crowd by immediately changing the colour of Sunderland's shorts from white to the traditional black, there was no disgrace in that. The new manager had barely had time to work with the team prior to the Burnley game so in some respects this was his first test, away to a side level on points with Sunderland, too close to the bottom of the second division for comfort.

Had Sunderland lost at Portsmouth would the Stokoe stardust have sparkled as it did from there on? Or would Sunderland have continued to struggle, especially as defeat would have extended the winless run into double figures, a dismal spell that began with a 5-1 reverse at Oxford United? With three minutes to go at Portsmouth, Sunderland were trailing 2-1. As the final whistle sounded they had won 3-2. Confidence was boosted, the new man had made a good start and by the time Sunderland lost again nine games later they were starting to head in the right direction in the league and had reached the fifth round of the most glorious cup run any side has ever made. They had also brought in the three extra players who would complete the cup team. Eight of the side who won at Pompey would have FA Cup winners' medals come the end of the season. Just 5,841 shivered their timbers in the December air of the historic city that houses *H.M.S. Victory,* come Wembley Sunderland would be watched by 100,000 plus millions on worldwide TV and supporters would kiss anyone, never mind 'Hardy'.

With the clock on 87 minutes, Billy Hughes, a player with swashbuckling piratical looks, unlocked the buried treasure, stealing in to beat teenage keeper Graham Horn to make it 2-2. The loyal supporters who'd travelled the length of the country on the Supporters' Association coaches celebrated the snatching of a crucial point but that long journey home was made all the better when Bobby Kerr capped a terrific personal performance with a last-minute winner. Kerr would lift the cup at Wembley, his winner here lifted spirits.

Jim Montgomery

Fourteen years earlier Fratton Park had been the scene where Sunderland lost their top flight status for the first time ever. On this occasion it provided the first light on the red and white renaissance that would reverberate around the globe. "We got what we deserved," was the general feeling from the players as reported by the following week's Sunderland programme, 'The Roker Review'. As normal on a long winless run, not much had been going right for the club but things changed with the arrival of Stokoe and those two late, late goals by young Scots who had come through the ranks and would win the cup were crucial in providing belief.

Sunderland would play a goalless draw at home to Preston a week later and then not play for 18 days during which three games were postponed. That unscheduled break gave Stokoe the chance to get his ideas over to his players – Sunderland had a state-of-the-art indoor training facility at Washington at the time – and when Sunderland next played it was the new year and the first game of the cup run.

Pompey's young keeper Horn would keep a clean sheet against Sunderland later in the season for Luton (although he didn't play in the Sunderland v Luton cup quarter-final) but thankfully he was beaten three times at Portsmouth. The first of those was from a first half goal from Dave Watson. Converted from centre forward to centre half by caretaker manager Billy Elliott just prior to Stokoe's arrival, it was Watson's first goal of the season, one of only three he'd score in the league – he'd score more in the cup.

Watson's strike had seen Sunderland go in level at half-time against Portsmouth, a penalty from substitute Brian Lewis having beaten Monty, the only penalty Pompey would score all season. Managed by former Surrey cricketer and Chelsea striker Ron Tindall, the home side went ahead through Nicky Jennings and with the clock ticking down, looked to have secured their first home win since September.

The three-minute turnaround gave the Wearsiders their first win in ten games against Portsmouth and ended a run of five consecutive away defeats. More importantly it was the turning point when the sleeping giant of SAFC was finally and very belatedly stung into life.

v Manchester City 3-1

Roker Park, FA Cup 5th round replay
February 27th 1973. Attendance: 51,782

SUNDERLAND	MANCHESTER CITY	REFEREE
Montgomery	Corrigan	R. Tinkler,
Malone	Book	Boston
Guthrie	Donachie	
Horswill	Doyle	
Watson	Booth	
Pitt	Jeffries	
Kerr	Mellor	
Hughes	Bell	
Halom	Marsh	
Porterfield	Lee	
Tueart	Towers	
Unused sub: Chambers	*Unused sub:* Barratt	

THE FA CUP brought about the end of standing areas at top class football grounds in England. The tragic events of the Hillsborough disaster in 1989 made that inevitable. When Manchester City came to Roker Park for a cup replay in 1973 though the excitement of being part of a swaying mass of humanity in one of the biggest 'ends' anywhere was truly incredible. The Roker End which was my regular place held 23,000 – more than the entire ground's capacity after safety concerns saw two-thirds of the massive bank of terracing demolished, together with other stadium changes as the ground approached the end of its 99-year life. In '73 though when cup fever had taken hold, being part of a crowd moving as one in time with the rhythm of the game made you feel almost part of the action itself.

Whenever Sunderland attacked the crowd swayed with them, moving like the waves crashing on Roker beach half a mile away. People who were struggling to stay up in the crowd would be hoisted above the mass and passed down above the heads of teeming thousands to the St. John's ambulance volunteers at the front who

If the crush got too much for you you'd be passed over the heads of fellow supporters to the St. John's ambulance people at the front. This image is from the sixties rather than the City game but illustrates the technique.

would see to them. When the goals came I lost my dad for a while. As the crowd erupted you'd get carried maybe 20 or 30 yards from where you started and when you got your balance having concentrated on not going under the trampling feet heralding a goal from the H-bombers it was time to look around and try and spot the person you'd came to the match with so you could begin trying to inch back towards each other. It didn't matter who you were standing next to of course because they were all Sunderland supporters and you were all part of the Roker Roar.

Roker certainly roared that night. No one would be surprised if ships on the North Sea coast changed course upon hearing it. This was the game voted 'Match of the Century' by supporters when Roker closed in 1997 having been open since 1898. For me the match of the century would be the 5-4 v Arsenal in 1935 but it's not worth arguing about. It's like saying would you be disappointed with second choice out of Angelina Jolie and Cameron Diaz (or Johnny Depp and Colin Firth if you prefer).

Having needed replays to get past Notts County and a Reading side managed by Sunderland legend Charlie Hurley, the Lads were drawn away to cup favourites Manchester City. City had just disposed of Liverpool who would be league champions that season and had also knocked out League Cup holders Stoke. Phenomenal travelling support split into two huge swathes of Maine Road terracing had followed Sunderland to Manchester more in hope than expectation but such was Sunderland's scintillating performance that as the red and white army made its way back to the north east many were already convinced that this at last was Sunderland's year.

City's England centre forward Franny Lee was having none of it, arguing that class would tell in the replay. It did. Sunderland won 3-1. "We started well and after about ten minutes I remember thinking, 'God, we are going to thrash these'" remembers right back Dick Malone. "We are moving sweetly tonight, we are on fire. We were playing that well."

Sunderland's 'H-bombers' were Vic Halom and Billy Hughes. Halom had just signed (he'd previously played for Bob Stokoe at Charlton) and was making just his fourth appearance for the club. Hughes had been an FA Youth Cup winner with Sunderland and was top scorer in the 72/73 season. The pair would score all three goals in this replay, be the scorers in the semi and combine to create the chance for the only goal in the final.

The reigning world champions were Brazil. Arguably the greatest display ever produced by a team in the World Cup final was by them as they beat Italy 4-1 in 1970. The goal of that game was the fourth, superbly crafted by Pele and co for Carlos Alberto. Sunderland's first against City was almost a carbon copy – except that the final shot was better! Attacking the Fulwell End, Ian Porterfield started the move on the left. He brought in his full back Ron Guthrie who moved the ball on to Hughes. Crisply working the ball across the edge of the City box, the visitors were watching not playing. It wasn't that they were slow, they were an excellent side. It was simply that Sunderland were playing the football of the gods. This was the time that Sunderland were smiled on from above, this was their year, this was the only one of the 'big four' games in the cup run that was played at Sunderland and this was the goal that summed up that team and that cup run. Having got the ball back from Hughes, Porterfield fed

Ritchie Pitt goes close against City.

Bobby Kerr who laid it off for Halom coming in at just the same angle as Carlos Alberto had when receiving from Pele in the most recent World Cup final. Halom hit a shot as true as any Roker Park ever witnessed. At least they did witness it. City's England keeper never saw it as Halom's bombshell blasted across him and into the top corner of the net. "I'd really tonked it," says Halom who jokes: "Hughesy will tell you it was meant as a cross, but it wasn't. Joe Corrigan was in goal for Man City, and to this day if I ever see him he always greets me with 'Not you again!'"

That was it. The crowd went absolutely mental as the City slickers reeled just as Spurs and Man Utd had in the epics of the early sixties but while they escaped with draws from games Sunderland should have won, this time Sunderland would win.

Lee, Rodney Marsh and Cold Heseldon-born Colin Bell searched for an equaliser but it was Sunderland who scored next. 26 minutes had gone when Billy Hughes doubled Sunderland's advantage. Taking a Kerr throw in his stride, Hughes beat his marker Willie Donachie and fired past Corrigan.

At half-time Sunderland were still two goals to the good but inevitably a side of City's quality would put up a fight and they pulled a goal back eight minutes into the second half when Lee scored from close range after Bell headed on a Mike Doyle cross. Pushing hard for an equaliser, City threatened through Ian Mellor, Bell, Marsh, future Sunderland man Tony Towers and Lee, who brought a good save out of Montgomery. The Roker rearguard weren't about to crumble though and looked to hit City on the break.

Hughes had already gone close when he scored his second and Sunderland's third with 12 minutes remaining. As with the opening goal the move was begun by Porterfield. He won the ball and set ever willing Malone away down the right. As Halom latched onto Superdick's cross the ball broke to Dennis Tueart. Three years later Tueart would score a spectacular Wembley winner for City who he would later serve as a director but on this occasion his powerful shot could only be parried by Corrigan and as Hughes and Kerr gleefully

Vic Halom looks for another goal.

came in together to apply the finishing touch, Hughes got there first
to finish off City's rally. Donachie and Marsh went in the book in the
next five minutes as the dummies were spat out. They lost 5-1 at
Wolves the following weekend and took one point out of their next
six games having seen their season crash on Wearside.

Referee Mr. Tinkler had officiated at the first two of a three-game
cup epic with Leeds six years earlier, a 1967 tie in which the teenage
Bobby Kerr's leg was broken. Leeds weren't quite on the horizon yet
for Sunderland but Kerr was destined to lift the cup against them at
Wembley in 67 days' time. Fate was playing a part and they might as
well have inscribed Sunderland's name on the trophy as City travelled
home. Not many of the Sunderland supporters were going home. It
was party time and that party wouldn't stop until after the cup was
won.

v Arsenal 2-1

Hillsborough, FA Cup semi-final
April 7th 1973. Attendance: 55,000

SUNDERLAND	ARSENAL	REFEREE
Montgomery	Wilson	Mr. D. W. Smith,
Malone	Rice	Stonehouse
Guthrie	McNab	
Horswill	Storey	
Watson	Blockley (Radford)	
Pitt	Simpson	
Kerr	Armstrong	
Hughes	Ball	
Halom	George	
Porterfield	Kennedy	
Tueart	Kelly	
Unused sub: Chambers		

HAVING BECOME only the second team of the century to achieve the 'double' of league and cup two years earlier, Arsenal were bidding to become the first team to reach a Wembley cup final three years in a row having been runners-up to Leeds in 1972.

Despite the top class opposition which included World Cup winner Alan Ball, the flamboyant Charlie George, hard man Peter Storey and north easterners Ray Kennedy and George Armstrong, Sunderland were far from overawed. They'd seen off just as big names in the fifth round versus Manchester City and since beating fellow second division outfit Luton comfortably in the quarter-final had dropped just one point in four games and won back to back away matches for the first time in almost exactly two years, the second of which had been against Sheffield Wednesday on the Hillsborough turf where they were to meet the Gunners.

Manager Bob Stokoe had no injury problems. Starting from the first game with Manchester City in the fifth round, the same eleven would play in each cup tie until the trophy was won and in none of those games did Sunderland bring on a substitute. By now they were a well organised team who were brimming with confidence. The huge open Kop end was jam packed with Sunderland supporters who also dominated the supposed 'neutral' section and had sizeable pockets of fans in the Arsenal end too. Sunderland started the game attacking the Kop end and were soon on top. The effervescence for which they were becoming renowned saw hard man Peter Storey and fellow midfielders Eddie Kelly and Ball commit early fouls on Hughes, Porterfield and Kerr as Sunderland began on the front foot. Charlie George also fouled Monty as Arsenal tried to unsettle Sunderland but it was as if Arsenal were the underdogs trying to get in the faces of their opponents.

Arsenal were looking shaky especially at centre half where Jeff Blockley was struggling to contain Vic Halom who as usual was making a complete and utter nuisance of himself. Moments before Halom gave Sunderland a 19th minute lead, Gunners' goalie Bob Wilson was injured in saving from Mickey Horswill. He received attention and probably could have done with his teammates retaining possession for a minute or two, but almost immediately Horswill lifted a ball over the Londoners' defence giving Halom a chase with Blockley who also had blustery conditions to cope with. Blockley looked like a teenage mother trying to control a pram missing a wheel as Halom bore down on him. Halom himself absolves Blockley of the ridicule he suffered at the time: "Jeff Blockley got murdered unfairly afterwards," says Vic. "He tried a back pass to Bob Wilson in goal, and I just latched onto it and knocked it in. The thing is it bobbled as I hit it and it went in off my ankle bone. For a moment I thought I'd missed it." Unlike Vic's goal in the fifth round against Man City this one might not have been out of 'the Pele book of Brazil classics' but it counted just the same and Sunderland were a goal ahead in the semi-final.

Soon afterwards Storey went in the book for a foul on Hughes as Sunderland continued to ask all the questions. Arsenal went close themselves with an Armstrong shot that clipped the outside of the post but Sunderland would hit the woodwork too when an inswinging Hughes corner almost went in only to hit the top of the bar. Halom continued to threaten, forcing Wilson into a good save and seeing Blockley desperately hack another goalbound effort clear. Wilson had been by far the busier keeper but Monty had had to make a tremendous save from Felling-born Armstrong before the half-time whistle sounded, moments after Halom had his name taken for having had a bit too much to say for himself.

Knowing how Manchester City had come at them in the second half of the fifth round replay when Sunderland had a two rather than one goal lead, Stokoe's men were braced to withstand whatever was going to come their way but it wasn't in the side's nature to defend. Sunderland were an attacking team and they were going to keep looking for another goal themselves.

In the heart of the Sunderland defence Dave Watson was illustrating why people were beginning to tout him for an England call-up while alongside him Ritchie Pitt was just as defiant. Pitt had been on loan at Arsenal earlier in the season and on the point of leaving Sunderland. He came back to keep new signing David Young out of the side and the semi was possibly his best game.

When the teams had been announced Sunderland supporters had been delighted that Arsenal had left their top scorer John Radford on the bench but after the Gunners' initial second-half surge had been repelled they brought on Radford in place of the beleaguered Blockley as they went for the equaliser. Within a few minutes of Radford's introduction though Sunderland doubled their lead and as with the first goal, success followed an injury to Wilson. The Arsenal keeper hurt himself blocking a shot from Hughes and needed attention before play resumed. Hughes had got a goal from a throw in against Manchester City and would do so again here. This time, Kerr launched a long throw which Tueart back-headed for Hughes to climb and plant a looping header over the despairing Wilson's dive and into the far corner.

Had sending offs been as prevalent in 1973 as they are now Arsenal would have soon been down to ten men but the already booked Storey escaped with just the concession of a free kick when he cynically felled the clean-through Hughes five yards from the edge of the box, the speed merchant having been released by his fellow H-bomber Halom.

Sunderland threatened to extend their lead, Tueart and Hughes testing Wilson as the bookings mounted, Malone, Guthrie and George having their names taken, the latter two after squabbling with each other.

Sunderland looked Wembley bound but no one was taking anything for granted especially when Arsenal pulled a goal back with six minutes to go. Monty got a hand to Charlie George's powerful shot and though he took the sting off it, the ball agonisingly crept just over the line. With massed ranks of the red and white army behind Monty's goal the Lads defended stoutly as the clock went on go-slow but as the final whistle sounded with Arsenal about to take a corner there were tears of joy.

Sunderland had become the first second division side to reach the cup final since Preston in 1964 but while Preston had lost then just as they'd lost to Sunderland in '37, the Lads were going to Wembley to win. When the news came through that the cup final opponents would be deadly rivals Leeds, who had beaten Wolves, lips were licked that little bit extra.

Wearing a white shirt rather than the red tracksuit he'd sport against his old enemy Don Revie at Wembley, Stokoe – by now called 'The Messiah' – came out to take the acclaim as it sunk in... Sunderland were in the cup final.

That night Rod Stewart and the Faces performed at 'The Rink' in Sunderland, a concert John Peel claimed was the greatest he ever saw. The Sunderland party that began after Man City were beaten in the fifth round was by now in full swing.

v Leeds United 1-0

Wembley, FA Cup final
May 5th 1973. Attendance: 100,000

SUNDERLAND	LEEDS UNITED	REFEREE
Montgomery	Harvey	Mr. K. Burns,
Malone	Reaney	Stourbridge
Guthrie	Cherry	
Horswill	Bremner	
Watson	Madeley	
Pitt	Hunter	
Kerr	Lorimer	
Hughes	Clarke	
Halom	Jones	
Porterfield	Giles	
Tueart	Gray (Yorath)	
Unused sub: Young		

APPARENTLY THE rest of the country thought Leeds would win. What did they know? Heading through the Leeds area on midnight departure coaches from Sunderland, the red and white army found plenty of Yorkshire revellers holding up five fingers on one hand and the thumb and forefinger of the other indicating a nil as they offered their predictions of the cup final score. Sunderland supporters were confident but not of such a big score-line. Two nil appeared to be the advice they were offering the Leeds fans.

In fact there were some very good judges tipping Sunderland against the defending cup holders who also had a European Cup Winners' Cup final later that month with A.C. Milan. Sunderland in contrast had played at Orient on the Monday before Wembley and had outstanding fixtures away to Cardiff and home to QPR to come in the next four days.

Just to be in the cup final would have been a dream for Sunderland given that they'd been near the bottom of the second division shortly before Christmas. For the opposition to be Don Revie's Leeds was extra special. "When Leeds United were mentioned on Wearside during the sixties and early seventies there would inevitably be an immediate intake of breath," says Sunderland's record outfield appearance maker and former manager Len Ashurst. Sunderland's cup final skipper Bobby Kerr had had his leg broken in a controversial three-game cup epic with Leeds in 1967, Willie McPheat – hero of the 1961 Spurs cup tie – had had his leg broken against Leeds in 1962 and never played for the club again and the following 1963/64 season when Leeds pipped Sunderland for the second division title as both were promoted are described as "near blood baths" by Ashurst who "liked a tackle" himself so was the ideal man to take on Revie's Leeds.

Sunderland manager Bob Stokoe loathed Leeds manager Don Revie, a former Sunderland player. They had been on opposite sides in the 1955 FA Cup final, Stokoe as Newcastle's centre half and Revie as Manchester City's deep lying centre forward with Stokoe coming out on top. It was Stokoe's claim that when he was player/manager of Bury Revie offered him a bribe to take it easy in a game that was vital to Leeds. If another former Sunderland centre forward, Brian Clough,

The teams arrive.

detested Revie, Stokoe loathed the Leeds supremo even more. "As we walked out [onto the Wembley pitch] Don Revie was next to me," described Stokoe. "He turned to me and said something along the lines of 'Revenge is sweet Stokoe.' There were a few unnecessary expletives in his statement." At the close of the afternoon after his now iconic run to greet Monty – a moment celebrated in the Stokoe statue outside the Stadium of Light – the Sunderland manager revealed: "I wanted to go up to Revie and look him in the eye and say 'Revenge is sweet, Revie; cheats never prosper' but I refrained from doing that and left it until later when it would have more impact, when the FA Cup would be in my hands."

Whichever way you looked at it this wasn't simply the fairytale cup final. Football supporters around the globe were tuning in and being fed rubbish about it being a 'David & Goliath' clash. From the Team of All The Talents, through the Charlie Buchan team of 1912/13, the glory days of the thirties and the glamour of the – albeit trophyless – fifties, Sunderland had always been a much bigger outfit than Leeds whose record gate was boosted by the masses of the red and white army. Sunderland were at Wembley to lift the cup and settle a few old scores with a team whose rivalry with Sunderland was and is second only to that of the rivalry with Newcastle.

Not many outside Wearside gave Sunderland a chance. No second division team had won the cup since 1931 and no team without a full international had won it since 1912. There were a couple of good judges who backed Sunderland though: Brian Clough, the ex Sunderland man who would of course take over disastrously from Revie at Leeds the following year and the legendary Bill Shankly at Liverpool. Shanks knew what Sunderland could do – he'd played against them on the only other occasion Sunderland had won the cup. That had been in 1937 and as everyone in red and white bunting bedecked Sunderland would tell you, '73 was just '37 with the numbers reversed.

Rain on the morning of the match had made the pitch quick but lots of players slipped and slid on the greasy surface. It was also a good excuse for Ritchie Pitt to almost snap England striker Allan Clarke in two early on: "Sorry ref – it's the pitch." Sunderland were there to win not be gallant whipping boys.

In the games against Man City and Arsenal, the youngest member of the Sunderland team, Mick Horswill, had been detailed to cancel out the work of the man who made the opposition midfield tick. First Colin Bell and then Alan Ball had been largely nullified by Horswill. No mean feat and at Wembley he stopped Johnny Giles dictating the game. Tactically Stokoe had Revie sussed. Winger Eddie Gray was meant to have the beating of right back Dick Malone but Malone had a stormer, curtailing his natural attacking game to look after Gray with Bobby Kerr doubling up when necessary. Leeds took Gray off.

With Tueart and Hughes running the legs off Leeds, Watson imperious at the back and Ian Porterfield – rejected by Leeds as a youngster – stroking the ball around, Sunderland gave as good as they got, Horswill shooting narrowly wide early on.

In the 31st minute Sunderland scored. United keeper Harvey thought it prudent to tip a high ball from Kerr over the bar as Hughes pressurised him. Hughes took the resultant corner, and with the Leeds defence preoccupied with the threat of Watson, Halom

Porterfield 1-0!

managed to steer the ball in the direction of Porterfield: "I could see it all the way. It was mine," said Porterfield. "I brought the ball down on my left thigh and as it dropped I hit it right footed with all my strength from 12 yards. Even as I connected I knew it was a goal. The shot was true and straight as an arrow....the ball crashed through the desperately outstretched arms of Harvey and high into the net. What a magical moment. Our fans, penned behind Harvey's goal, must have seen it all the way. They went mad."

Horswill came in for some rough treatment from Giles and Billy Bremner but kept his discipline well, he wasn't going to be lured into little battles that would take his focus off his job. That was true of every man in the team.

Sunderland were good value for their half-time lead and as the teams reappeared from the Wembley tunnel captain Kerr walked to the massed ranks of the red and white army behind the goal. He whirled his arms round and round to urge them to be the twelfth man. It wasn't necessary because no one intended going home having not shouted themselves hoarse but it transmitted the feeling that everyone was in this together. 'Ha'way the Lads' boomed around the stadium as did the Blaydon Races – Blaydon is south of the Tyne remember and in 1973 was still part of County Durham.

Malone cleared after Monty parried a Bremner shot early on, he'd later have to clear again after an unforgettable moment. Sunderland weren't about to sit back though. That wasn't Stokoe's Stars' style. In one attack Hughes and Porterfield had shots blocked before full back Guthrie shot into the side netting and soon afterwards Guthrie was close again with a piledriver from outside the box.

Then in the 65th minute Jim Montgomery made the greatest save ever seen at Wembley, effectively ensuring the cup would have red and white ribbons. Monty takes up the story: "Paul Reaney knocked it towards the far post where Trevor Cherry got past Dick Malone and headed back across me. I was going one way and had to start going the other way to reach it, but I managed to palm it out. As I was on the ground I saw the ball go to a white shirt. I used my instinct to get up and make the save. I got my hand to it and pushed it up where it hit the bar." Malone completed the clearance and is still livid he had to: "Allan Clarke had actually tripped me because when the ball was coming across to Trevor Cherry I could have headed it clear but he tripped me... I felt if that had gone in I'd have chinned the referee."

TV commentators thought it was in but the fans behind the goal were used to seeing Monty make unbelievable saves; this one just happened to be seen by millions in the cup final. "Jimmy, Jimmy Monty lalalalalala" emanated from the fans. Leeds had given it their best shot and it hadn't been good enough. "At that moment I could feel it deep down in my belly," said Ian Porterfield. "We couldn't lose. Leeds would never score. And they must have felt the same."

Sunderland's name had been on the FA Cup since the fifth round. Never had 'And now you're going to believe us, we're gonna win the cup' been sung with more feeling. 25 minutes later – during which Sunderland came closer to scoring than Leeds – the cup had been won. Stokoe ran across the pitch to Monty, Sunderland won their only major trophy since the war and on BBC radio, commentators who'd covered dozens of cup finals admitted: "You've never seen scenes like this." It was Sunderland's cup. The Messiah had delivered but as Stokoe said himself; "I didn't bring the magic. It was always there. I just came back to find it."

Bobby Kerr receives the cup.

v Vasas Budapest 2-0

Nep Stadium, European Cup Winners'
Cup 1st Rd 1st leg. September 19th
1973. Attendance: 35,000

SUNDERLAND	VASAS BUDAPEST	REFEREE
Montgomery	Meszaros	Mr. F.S.M. Lobo
Malone	Torok	
Guthrie	Fabian	
Horswill	Kantor	
Watson	Lakinger (Gass)	
Pitt	Vidats	
Kerr	Muller	
Hughes	Toth	
Halom (Young)	Varadi	
Porterfield	Kovac	
Tueart	Sipocz	
Unused subs:		
Swinburne,		
Lathan, McGivern.		

PARTICIPATION IN the European Cup Winners' Cup as FA Cup winners took Sunderland to the capital of Hungary for their first taste of a major European competition. Vasas Budapest had a fine European pedigree having played in played in the European Cup in five of its 18 seasons. They had been quarter finalists in 1967/68 going out to Benfica who reached the Wembley final against Manchester United, while in 1957/58 Vasas had reached the semi-finals only to succumb to the all-conquering Real Madrid.

Bob Stokoe selected the same eleven who had won the FA Cup for this prestigious game and they were far too good for Vasas. Sunderland played really well, deservedly winning 2-0 with a 68th-minute header by Billy Hughes from a searching Dick Malone cross and an 89th minute wonder goal from Dennis Tueart.

Tueart got the ball on the halfway line and tore through the home defence, slaloming past three defenders before beating keeper Meszaros. At the other end Sunderland's defence coped well with what the home side had to offer. Only Bela Varadi, who had netted a hat-trick in the Hungarian Cup final against local rivals Honved, offered any serious threat to Dave Watson, who in the week he made his European debut was also called up to the full England squad for the first time.

The match was played in Budapest's Nep Stadium rather than Vasas' own ground, the Vasas SC Stadium. This was normal in Hungary where showpiece matches were often staged at the 'Nepstadion'. Sunderland's visit was part of a double header as prior to the Sunderland game Ferencvaros took on Gwardia Warsaw in a UEFA Cup game which the Polish side won 1-0. Surrounded by a running track and minus floodlights the 100,000 capacity ground was never as much as a third full with the published attendance being the joint attendance for the two games. Most Ferencvaros fans left before the Sunderland game and of the 500 or so Sunderland fans who travelled most got there shortly before the Sunderland match,

Billy Hughes in again in the home leg against Vasas Budapest.

Ritchie Pitt

unaware that their ticket would have also got them into the earlier fixture.

Although the match was Sunderland's first serious European game, Sunderland had participated in the Anglo Italian Cup in the summers of 1972 and 1970, playing a total of four competitive matches in Italy. The European Cup Winners' Cup though was the real thing and while now defunct, in its time it was the second most important European trophy, ranked higher than the UEFA Cup, hence Sunderland and Vasas having top billing of the two games played at the Nep that night.

The trip to Budapest proved to be particularly noteworthy for two players: Ritchie Pitt and Vic Halom. Pitt had a fine game, defending stoutly in helping Sunderland claim a clean sheet. Just a month short of his 22nd birthday and already with close to 150 games under his belt and a cup winners' medal to his name, this would be the Ryhope lad's last full 90 minutes. Three days later he was injured in a clash with Luton's John Ryan in a second division match and never played again. Pitt later had a joint testimonial with fellow injury victim Bobby Park against Dutch side AZ and took up a career in teaching.

For Halom the trip to Budapest gave him the opportunity to meet some of his family for the first time. Vic's father, Louis, was from Budapest as were some of his uncles and he explains: "I met my aunties there for the first time." However Halom had lost all his front teeth in a clash in Sunderland's match at Oxford the previous weekend and as Sunderland had flown to Hungary on the Monday he'd not been able to visit a dentist: "So I met my Aunty Elizabeth at the Nep stadium. She said, 'Which one's Vic Halom?' and when she saw me with no front teeth she nearly passed out. She must have been thinking 'What an ugly kid he is'."

Sunderland rewarded their fans by doubling prices to £2 and £1 for the second leg, the reason given being that it was to help pay for the upgrade in floodlighting to help colour television coverage of European games. It didn't go down well and inevitably knocked thousands off the gate. Sunderland would win the second leg 1-0 courtesy of a Tueart penalty to go through 3-0 on aggregate.

Defeat at Roker brought back bad memories for Vasas manager Lajos Baroti. Seven years earlier he'd been in charge of the Hungarian national side who lost a World Cup quarter-final to the USSR at Roker.

v Sporting Lisbon 2-1

Roker Park, European Cup Winners'
Cup 2nd Rd 1st leg.
October 24th 1973. Attendance: 31,568

SUNDERLAND	SPORTING LISBON	REFEREE
Montgomery	Damas	Mr. Kitabdjian,
Malone	Manaca	France
Bolton	Periera	
Horswill	Fraguito	
Watson	Laranjeiro	
Young	Alhinho	
Kerr	Chico	
Hughes	Nelson	
Halom	Yazalde	
Porterfield	Wagner	
Tueart	Nando	
Unused subs: Lathan,	*Unused subs:* Fernando,	
Swinburne, Mitchell,	Tinhal, Baltazak, Bastos,	
McGiven, Ellison	Tome	

THE VISIT of former European Cup Winners' Cup holders Sporting Lisbon provided a new challenge for Sunderland, whose line-up was the one that had won the FA Cup other than for a changed left side of the defence. Finished by injury, Ritchie Pitt had been replaced by David Young while at left back, up-and-coming Joe Bolton was in the process of replacing veteran Ron Guthrie.

Sporting's plans were disrupted by three of their players being arrested for shoplifting on Tyneside. Horrified by the disgrace brought upon their proud club, Sporting sent the trio home on the first flight, the thieves being fined by Newcastle magistrates when their case was subsequently heard.

Despite this Sunderland felt there was no justice as they were edged out over two legs of a tie where they could easily have made further progress, especially after being two goals to the good. The opener came after 32 minutes and it had a large touch of good fortune. Bolton began the move with a throw to Young who fed Halom. The big centre forward played in Bobby Kerr; Sunderland's

goal at the same stage in the FA Cup final had stemmed from a high ball from Kerr that the keeper took no risks with and flipped over the bar. On this occasion Kerr lofted in a high hanging centre from a wider position than he had at Wembley. Goalkeeper Damas thought he could catch what looked a tame ball but as he caught the ball at the Roker End he stepped over the goal line and the linesman signalled a goal. The visiting team surrounded the French referee in prolonged protest but the goal stood.

Moments before the goal Billy Hughes had been denied by a brilliant save from Damas and Mick Horswill had also gone close so Sunderland had claims to be worth their lead. Halom thought he'd doubled the advantage but this time the linesman came to Sporting's rescue, ruling out the striker's effort for a tight offside.

Sunderland knew a second leg in Lisbon would be tough and wanted at least a two goal cushion. Soon after half-time Dennis Tueart and Dave Watson both came close to extending the lead, but Sporting weren't just sitting back and were quick on the break, so Sunderland had to be wary of leaving themselves light at the back.

Montgomery had to pull out a good save to deny Chico and watched gratefully as a shot from Nando whistled wide. The second goal Sunderland needed though duly arrived thanks to two of the strongest runners in a hard working team. Captain Kerr gained possession on the right wing and whipped the ball over before Sporting could set themselves. Anchor-man Horswill had determination to match his youthful energy and just managed to get onto the cross a tiny fraction of a second before the keeper but it was enough. Horswill's effort found the back of the net as the 'keeper found Horswill, who was concussed and didn't realise it was him that had scored until after the match!

A third goal would have surely been enough to give Sunderland every chance of progressing into the quarter-finals but once again a flag ruled out another effort, this time Tueart thinking he'd maintained his record of scoring in every one of Sunderland's European games.

With five minutes to go disaster struck when Sporting got an away goal. It had a touch of inevitability about it as it came from Hector Yazalde who tucked away a close-range header from a Chico cross. Yazalde had seen a 19th-minute effort disallowed for offside and certainly knew where the

Vic Halom

back of the net was. He won the European Golden Shoe that season as the continent's top scorer with 46 goals. Yazalde won a car for winning the Golden Shoe but sold it and shared the money with his teammates. Nicknamed Chirola, he had been Argentina's Footballer of the Year in 1970 and would score twice more for Argentina in the World Cup finals at the end of this 73/74 season.

With a final – or 'half-time' – score of 2-1 Sunderland knew they'd have their work cut out and so it proved. Goals from Yazalde and Fraguito gave Lisbon a 3-2 aggregate victory although the 'Sporting' part of their name was called into question as they were subsequently fined by UEFA for unsporting conduct, their ball boys having disappeared once they were in front as they wound the clock down while Sunderland strove to prolong their European adventure.

The same two players had scored as they'd disposed of Welsh Cup winners Cardiff in the first round and they'd reach the semi-finals of the competition where they went out at the hands of eventual winners Magdeburg. Sporting would go on to win the Portuguese championship while Sunderland would miss out on promotion.

Their own success was destined to strangle Sunderland's ambitions as simply too many games in too few days proved too much. In the 14 days between the two legs of this tie with the Portuguese giants Stokoe's side played four games including two tough cup ties with Derby, one of which involved extra time. People weren't ready for squad rotation and there was disbelief on the terraces when Sunderland's team was announced at Hull City's Boothferry Park where Sunderland lost a league game on the Saturday before the second leg. Stokoe 'rested' his front five, Bobby Mitchell getting a debut, Rod Belfitt a first start and Ray Ellison making the bench for the only time in the league season.

Defeat at Hull left the cup holders fourteenth in the second division. 4-1 and 3-0 wins came in the week after European elimination and come the end of the campaign promotion had been missed by two points. The cup team had begun to break up with the sale of Tueart and Horswill added to the injury to Pitt. Sunderland's cup exploits had been fantastic but had promotion been secured perhaps, just perhaps, the rest of the seventies might have been even more sensational.

v Derby County 1-1

Roker Park,
League Cup 2nd round replay.
October 29th 1973. Attendance: 38,975

SUNDERLAND	DERBY COUNTY	REFEREE
Montgomery	Boulton	Mr. R. Tinkler,
Malone	Webster	Boston
Bolton	Nish	
Horswill	Newton	
Watson	McFarland	
Young	Todd	
Kerr (Belfitt)	McGovern (O'Hare)	
Hughes	Gemmill	
Halom	Davies	
Porterfield	Hector	
Tueart	Hinton	

WHEN IT comes to greatest games, this one deserves to be ranked with the best of them. Both teams were on top form and between them they served up as good a football match as you could ever wish to see. Summing up in the *Sunderland Echo*, 'Argus' wrote: "Wembley was no better than this. It was a bigger occasion and a great achievement but last night reached a peak which will be long remembered."

This was the middle match of a three game epic with Derby. Each of the three games were superb, Sunderland eventually coming out on top in the second replay but for a pure game of football this was a match that is still raved about by anyone who was there. Personally, I saw my 1,500th Sunderland game in 2010 and have had happier occasions and better results but ask me to pick the best game I've ever been to and this one would be the answer.

Since the original tie at Derby's old Baseball Ground Brian Clough and Peter Taylor had resigned at Derby. Now three weeks after the draw at Derby and two weeks after Clough's departure the Rams arrived at Roker under the direction of Dave Mackay – a veteran of the 1961 cup tie with Spurs.

Sunderland supporters at the away game at Derby had been disappointed by the fact that Dennis Tueart was missing from the cup winning team in addition to the absence of Ritchie Pitt who would never play again after his injury the previous month. Tueart's replacement, John Lathan, came to the fore scoring both Sunderland's goals in a pulsating tie that led to this replay.

Sunderland's European involvement had delayed the game. Clough later won the European Cup twice with Nottingham Forest and had gone close with Derby the year before, the Rams most controversially losing to Juventus in the semi-final. Derby had been league champions in 1972, would be again in '75 and were fourth when they came to Roker.

A record League Cup attendance of almost 39,000 turned out on a Monday night and right from a first-minute free kick that Derby centre forward Roger Davies had to clear there was non-stop action from two teams hell-bent on attack. The white-booted Alan Hinton was first to threaten for the visitors only to shoot over and soon afterwards Montgomery had to save from Archie Gemmill.

It was a first return to Roker for Colin Todd who'd been sold to Derby for a record £170,000 fee two and a half years earlier and 'Toddo' soon came to County's rescue, dispossessing the man who would surpass Todd's record as Sunderland's record sale, Dennis Tueart.

It was Tueart who won a penalty in the 20th minute. Freed by good work from Porterfield and Horswill, Tueart was brought down by visiting keeper Colin Boulton. Tueart took the spot kick himself only to be denied by a fine save. Moments later Boulton was beaten by his near namesake Joe Bolton only for Gemmill to clear the young Sunderland full back's shot off the line and soon afterwards Billy Hughes found the back of the net only to have his effort disallowed.

The Lads were piling on the pressure and it paid off on the half hour mark from a corner, Tueart making up for the penalty miss with an emphatic finish. Hughes then had another 'goal' disallowed

as Derby defended desperately to stay in the match as Sunderland peppered the visitors' goal.

Half-time couldn't come quickly enough for Mackay's men but they came out fighting after the break. Hinton and Gemmill had already threatened when Davies brought a fingertip save out of Monty.

With quarter of an hour left Derby introduced ex-Sunderland forward John O'Hare and within five minutes they were level after a determined run by the excellent Gemmill, who shrugged off two attempts to dispossess him by David Young, before drilling home the equaliser.

The start of extra time saw Rod Belfitt make his second appearance for Sunderland, coming on for Bobby Kerr as Sunderland pressed for a winner with Halom, Horswill and Watson all getting on the end of moves without finding the back of the net. Derby were going for it too, Henry Newton and Gemmill threatening before Davies shot into the side netting.

Neither team deserved to lose on the night but at least Sunderland won the toss for the right to stage the second replay and so 48 hours later all assembled to do it all over again. In another top class game Sunderland eventually came through. A second-half hat-trick from Halom, born

nine miles from Derby, took Sunderland through 3-0. The subtext here was that once again Sunderland centre half Dave Watson was immaculate while Halom bagged the match ball against the man keeping Watson out of the England side, Roy McFarland. That wouldn't remain the case for long as England would play just one more game before Watson made the breakthrough.

v Manchester Utd 2-3

Old Trafford, Division Two
November 30th 1974. Attendance: 60,585

SUNDERLAND	MANCHESTER UTD	REFEREE
Montgomery	Stepney	Mr. G. Hill,
Malone	Forsyth	Leicester
Guthrie	Houston	
Moncur	Greenhoff (Davies)	
Watson	Holton	
Porterfield	Buchan	
Kerr	Morgan	
Hughes	Pearson	
Halom (Finney)	McIlroy	
Robson	Macari	
Towers	Daly	

THIS SECOND division clash was watched by the biggest league gate in England for almost two years, Sunderland's massive travelling support pushing the gate to three thousand more than United had had for their biggest gate of the previous season in the higher division for their derby with Manchester City. The football lived up to the anticipation of the huge crowd as the match ebbed and flowed and though in the end the result went the home side's way, Sunderland could just as easily have won it had they had a little bit of luck.

It was a rare second tier game shown on *Match of the Day* in an era when normally highlights of just three games were shown but such was its quality the game was named 'Match of the Season' at the end of the campaign.

"Sunderland were magnificent against us," said United's Scottish international winger Willie Morgan who predicted: "They'll go up with us – no question about it." While Morgan was correct with the first part of that statement, unfortunately he was wrong with the latter part, Sunderland finishing fourth having lost two of their last three games when the top three went up.

HUGHES' FIRST

... AND SECOND

STEPNEY STEPS IN

At Old Trafford though they produced a display of attacking football that had the home fans reared on the likes of Charlton, Best and Law appreciating that Sunderland were a terrific team with some star players. "Billy Hughes is the most exciting forward in the country," proclaimed United's manager Tommy Docherty after seeing Hughesy score twice and run United ragged, ably supported by Sunderland-born Pop Robson, 24 games into the first of his three playing spells with the club just two seasons after being the top scorer in the top flight.

Second division or not, Manchester United still had top players, every one of them played full international football during their careers and they raced into an early lead. New £200,000 signing Stuart 'Pancho' Pearson tucked a well placed drive beyond Monty at the old 'Scoreboard End' in front of the visiting supporters as the home side capitalised on a positive start.

Sunderland had played some very big games since their last visit to Manchester 21 months earlier when a 2-2 draw at City signalled the take off for the cup run and all that followed. On that occasion Billy Hughes had put Sunderland ahead and he would do so again only this time he had to equalise first. It didn't take him long, Sunderland; clad in all white with a red and black stripe down the sleeves, slipped effortlessly into top gear and blew United away as if they'd brought the North Sea wind across the Pennines with them.

It could have been three. United had a sole survivor of the team that had become the first English team to win the European Cup six years earlier, goalkeeper Alex Stepney. In that final against Benfica at Wembley he'd produced a crucial block to deny Eusebio a late winner before United romped home in extra time. Here he saved his side again, spreading himself to thwart Pop Robson moments before the break. That's not to say Sunderland would have won if 3-1 up at Old Trafford – Monty in goal at the other end would bear testament to that having seen 3-1 with four minutes left become 3-3 a decade earlier. Nonetheless Robson was a clinical finisher and the save was a key moment.

Sunderland looked to have weathered United's second-half surge when they got a stroke of luck ten minutes after the restart. An equaliser was awarded even though it was blatantly obvious that Sammy McIlroy was offside as Sunderland pushed out. As Morgan's shot found the back of the net there was disbelief that the goal was given. In 2010 it wouldn't be debatable what with first phase, second phase, active and inactive interpretations of Law 11. In 1974 though McIlroy was simply offside and the goal should have been disallowed.

Manchester United had long been global news and even had a player named after a German newspaper – Gerry Daly setting up the winner for McIlroy.

It was the biggest league gate to watch Sunderland since a last day of the season trip to the same ground in 1968 when the Lads stunned the home side by winning 2-1, costing United their chance of the title just three weeks before Bobby Charlton and co won the European Cup. Since then Sunderland too had enjoyed cup glory and offered the Stretford End a reminder.

Although there had been a full season between Sunderland's FA Cup win and this fixture, the United fans taunted 'Oh how'd you win the cup?' after they took an early lead. Within a few minutes after Stepney had twice been beaten by Hughes the retort came, 'That's how we won the cup.' At Old Trafford that November afternoon there were still eight members of the cup team playing but that was soon to become seven. A week later after one of his best ever performances as Portsmouth were hammered 4-1 at Roker Park, Ian Porterfield suffered horrendous injuries in a car crash. Though the cup final goalscorer came back for half a season the following year he was never the same player. Having already lost two members of the cup team to the other side of Manchester (Tueart and Horswill having joined City) and Pitt to injury, in some respects it can be argued that this was the 'cup' team's last big performance. With promotion missed on the final day of the season Dave Watson and Ron Guthrie departed and the era was at an end.

v **Bolton Wanderers 2-0**

Roker Park, Division Two

April 19th 1976. Attendance: 51,983

SUNDERLAND	BOLTON W	REFEREE
Montgomery	Siddall	Mr. C. Seel,
Malone	Walsh	Carlisle
Bolton	Nicholson	
Towers	Greaves	
Ashurst	Jones P.	
Moncur	Allardcye	
Kerr	Morgan	
Train	Whitmore	
Holton	Jones G. (Byrom)	
Robson	Reid	
Greenwood (Hughes)	Thompson	

HAVING WON the FA Cup within six months of becoming Sunderland manager, Bob Stokoe had found promotion harder to achieve but on this sunny Easter Monday 'The Messiah' took Sunderland back into the Promised Land. It was only the second time the Lads had ever won promotion and the following Saturday relegated Portsmouth would sportingly form a 'Guard of Honour' as Sunderland took to the pitch before chalking up another victory to win the second division title for the first time. Indeed it was the only time that particular trophy has come to the town where the second division was formed. Subsequent times Sunderland have been champions of England's second tier the trophy has been the old championship trophy.

The man who would steer Sunderland to that title twenty years later and again three years after that was in the visiting side, a young Peter Reid. Two of his Bolton teammates would later play for Sunderland; goalkeeper Barry Siddall who succeeded Monty before the end of the calendar year and Sam Allardyce who came to Sunderland twice, firstly as a player and later as a youth coach when Reid was in charge.

Joe Bolton

Promotion was entirely based on home form: 19 wins, two draws and no defeats was what Roker fans expected. However there had been a shock the previous month when third division Crystal Palace won an FA Cup quarter-final in the strongest of winds, Palace manager Malcolm Allison duly gaining revenge for seeing his Man City side defeated three years earlier.

Sunderland were to make no such mistake against Bolton. With three games left Sunderland were four points clear of fourth-place

Wanderers with three to go up and still two points for a win. Victory would mean Bolton couldn't catch the Lads and promotion would be won. Both sides had scored four times 48 hours earlier, Sunderland 4-1 at Hull where Gary Rowell scored his first career goal while Bolton thumped Oldham 4-0.

Nerves were to the fore early on with play scrappy but Sunderland were to take the lead in the same minute they had when winning the FA Cup. Thirty-one had elapsed when Bobby Kerr whacked the ball past Barry Siddall but the celebrations were doused as players and supporters realised that the referee had awarded Sunderland a penalty rather than a goal! Midfielder Ray Train, playing his tenth game after being transferred from Carlisle, had been brought down by Roy Greaves. Thankfully Tony Towers converted his fourth penalty of the season.

Wanderers' Willie Morgan had predicted Sunderland would go up the season before when he'd been part of the Manchester United side in the previous 'Greatest Game'. He was a year out with his prediction and took his life in his hands when being booked for a foul on Joe Bolton. The Sunderland full back was renowned as a hard man and their battle was one of the game's key clashes.

On the opposite wing for the visitors was former Liverpool and England man Peter Thompson who could threaten any defence so despite their home record Sunderland had to be wary of the Wanderers' threat. Sunderland though were dominating and doubled their lead before half-time.

Top scorer Pop Robson was always on the move in the box and reading a Bobby Kerr centre he made sure he was in the right place at the right time to clinically despatch a header past Siddall.

125 league games had been played between the 1973 FA Cup final and this promotion clincher. The Lads were finally going up and the mood on the terraces was as much of relief as of delight although that was there aplenty. Towers would make his England debut less than three weeks later and along with the twin engines of Kerr and Train, Sunderland dominated midfield despite the graft of

Pop Robson turns to celebrate his goal.

the talented young Reid for whom this game would leave an indelible imprint.

There was a moment's worry when Montgomery was injured but sub Billy Hughes was undaunted, warming up with the prospect of going in goal. He'd kept a clean sheet having taken over in goal against Chesterfield the previous season. Even when big Sam Allardyce headed home a Morgan free kick with twelve minutes left there was confidence that the Lads would complete the job, although the final whistle was still pleaded for by over 50,000 budding Roger Whittakers.

This was the last time Roker Park held in excess of 50,000, the capacity gradually being reduced in the old ground's last two decades. The previous league gate of over 50,000 had been for a derby with Newcastle in the fourth-last home game before relegation six years earlier. Monty, Kerr and Hughes had played in that game. They'd seen a hell of a lot since then but the journey was over and Sunderland were back in the big time.

v **Newcastle Utd** 4-1

St. James' Park, Division Two

February 24th 1979. Attendance: 34,733

SUNDERLAND	NEWCASTLE UTD	REFEREE
Siddall	Hardwick	Mr. P. Partridge,
Henderson	Brownlie	Cockfield,
Bolton	Nattress	Co. Durham
Arnott (Docherty)	Martin	
Clarke	Bird	
Elliott	Blackley (Mitchell)	
Chisholm	Shoulder	
Rostron	Walker	
Entwistle	Withe	
Lee	Hibbert	
Rowell	Connolly	

DERBY GAMES are always hugely anticipated and fiercely fought but are often forgotten as scrappy games of few goals merge into each other in the memory. The exceptions though are burned onto the brain like tattoos of the mind. Great wins and awful defeats become defining moments in a lifetime's support for a club and great wins in derby games become the touchstone by which fans keep the faith when faith is severely tested…and Sunderland have pushed the boundaries of their supporters' devotion more than most clubs would get away with!

To play your greatest rivals off the park on their own patch is the stuff of dreams. There have been numerous wins on Tyneside since this one including the all important 1990 play-off game but none of the subsequent St. James' successes have been as comprehensive as this laying waste of all things black and white.

Only three players have scored a century of goals for Sunderland since World War Two. One of them was a local lad and this was the day he scored the three goals supporters remember more than the other 100 he netted: Gary Rowell. "In one of my last in a long line of interviews, someone said to me, 'Gary, would it be fair to say that this

The Football Echo *celebrates a famous victory.*

means more to you because you hate Newcastle?' and I said 'Yeah.' I didn't actually say the words 'I hate Newcastle', I just said 'Yeah' but in some of the morning papers it was plastered all over the pages. It's true but it might not be the wisest thing I've ever done saying it in public."

Gary wasn't going to be popular on Tyneside anyway and probably wouldn't have been happy if he was ...but his status on Wearside where he was already hugely revered became sky high and has never waned. Over three decades on Rowell still summarises Sunderland games on local radio, has a column in the *Sunderland Echo* and still is serenaded with renditions of 'We all live in a Gary Rowell World' at just about every game. And rightly so! Gary Rowell is a red and white legend not least for this hat-trick and is Sunderland to the core.

Sunderland went into this game as promotion chasers in fifth place in the second division (when only two went up and there were no play-offs) while the Magpies were marooned in mid-table. It took Sunderland just six minutes to stamp their authority on the game, Rowell lunging at a loose ball in the box after Jeff Clarke's free kick was flicked on by Gordon Chisholm and then Wilf Rostron to unhinge the home rearguard. It was typical of Gary's goals. He was the master of converting the half chance. If there was a loose ball in the box Rowell was onto it quicker than a night club Lothario pouncing on a woman. Playing in midfield as often as he operated up front, the Sunderland man made an art of ghosting into the box unnoticed, arriving in the right place at the right time and simply slotting the ball into the net with the minimum of fuss. Rowell's talent was in making the most difficult part of the game appear simple.

Gary Rowell completes his hat trick from the penalty spot.

If Rowell's opener was a classic poacher's goal his second was simply a classic. Sent clear by his former youth team colleague and Newcastle-supporting Kevin Arnott, Rowell waited for home keeper Steve Hardwick to commit himself before sliding the ball home with the confidence of a player to whom scoring was second nature: "I just knocked a ball through for Gary and he finished it off…he had the knack of being in the right place at the right time, especially for a midfield player," remembers Arnott while Rowell recalls: "Kevin Arnott picked me out with a great through ball for the second goal. I'd played with Kev for years and years – we played together as kids, so we had a great understanding of each other's game."

Hardwick denied Rowell claiming the match ball before half-time with a smart save giving Newcastle manager Bill McGarry an opportunity to rally his troops at the interval. McGarry would later damn Rowell with faint praise: "Rowell is quite simply a gift. You never see him he just scores goals." Certainly McGarry's defence didn't see him!

Inevitably the home side had a spell on top and pulled a goal back five minutes into the second half when John Connolly headed in Nigel Walker's floated free kick. The set piece had been conceded by Mick Henderson but the Newbiggin lad made amends just twelve minutes later when he won a penalty after being brought down by Sunderland-born Newcastle substitute Kenny Mitchell. Rowell is arguably the best penalty taker in Sunderland's history. He scored 20 out of the 21 he took, routinely rolling the ball right into either corner having often sent the keeper the wrong way and he appeared to be ice cool as he strode up to score, side-footing the ball to the keeper's left but appearances can be deceptive: "A lot of people say that I looked really cool taking that penalty but I was anything but. My stomach was really churning…The penalty was the key moment in the game. It was such a relief for it to go in. Looking back I'm actually pleased it was in front of the Newcastle fans because I'd really stuck one up them. For a Sunderland lad it doesn't get much better than that."

Newcastle's fightback was over. They collapsed leaving Sunderland to toy with them in the final half hour. Referee Pat Partridge appeared to take pity on them, disallowing a Bob Lee 'goal' for the visitors to bring play back…for a free kick to Sunderland! The fourth goal wasn't long in arriving though, Rowell turning provider creating a 72nd minute goal for Wayne Entwistle to head home and complete the rout. Not only was it 4-1, it was a score-line that was fully deserved from start to finish. Sunderland were comprehensively the better team and in Rowell had a red and white hero who had well and truly rubbed it in.

v West Ham Utd 2-0

Roker Park, Division Two
May 12th 1980. Attendance: 47,129

SUNDERLAND	WEST HAM UTD	REFEREE
Turner	Parkes	Mr. J. B. Worral,
Whitworth	Stewart	Warrington
Hinnigan	Brush	
Chisholm	Bonds	
Hindmarch	Martin	
Elliott	Devonshire	
Arnott	Neighbour	
Buckley	Pearson (Holland)	
Hawley	Cross	
Robson	Brooking	
Cummins (Dunn)	Pike	

48 HOURS after winning the FA Cup, West Ham fulfilled an outstanding league fixture at Roker Park. Nine of their Wembley heroes played with Jimmy Neighbour and Paul Brush coming into the side in place of Paul Allen and Frank Lampard Snr. Originally scheduled for February 2nd, the match had been postponed giving the Hammers the length of the country to travel when a right old Cockney knees up was what they'd have preferred after beating Arsenal on the Saturday.

When Sunderland had won the cup seven years earlier they too had had a Monday night away game to play, in Sunderland's case at Cardiff where a draw had enabled Bob Stokoe's old Newcastle teammate Jimmy Scoular's side to escape relegation. Two nights later the season had been signed off in controversial fashion against QPR at Roker when the visiting keeper had played a blinder. That keeper, Phil Parkes, now stood between Sunderland and promotion in goal for West Ham.

The Hammers had nothing but pride to play for but as newly-crowned cup holders they had plenty of that and were still on a high after Wembley: "We couldn't get the ball off them for the

Pop Robson fires in a shot on goal against his old team.

first 20 minutes," admits Kevin Arnott, scorer of the first goal that night.

Having missed out on promotion a year earlier after seeing Crystal Palace win after their own fixtures were complete, Sunderland this time knew that a point would guarantee them promotion. Moreover they were unbeaten at home, had the tightest home defence in the league and by the end of the night would be the top home scorers.

The gates were closed at Roker Park with just over 47,000 inside and thousands more locked out. "The whole build up was unreal," remembers Arnott. "We went out for something to eat in Sunderland before the match and then had to get a police escort to get the coach to the ground because, even at this time between 5 and 6 o'clock the place was crammed and everything was blocked."

With West Ham relaxed against anxious Sunderland, Trevor Brooking and Alan Devonshire confidently stroked the ball around early on but centre forward David Cross twice wasted good opportunities. When Sunderland got forward themselves Parkes made excellent saves from Shaun Elliott and Pop Robson as supporters wondered what it would take to beat him. Arnott had the answer, calmly placing the ball out of the keeper's reach when another Elliott effort was parried. Going a goal up ten minutes before half-time calmed Sunderland down. They knew a point was sufficient and that even if they conceded one they would be okay. Freed from the overbearing worry of slipping up they began to play as they could and suddenly it was the Hammers who were chasing the ball and after their weekend exertions they weren't in much of a state to do so.

A second goal was wanted but as long as Chris Turner maintained his clean sheet nerves would stay settled. Turner had only been beaten twice in the previous seven home games and in front of him the defence was looking solid. Midway

Bryan Robson

through the second half the visitors went down to ten men when Ray Stewart went off injured after they'd already used their sub and as the game went into the closing stages it seemed as if the Hammers were happy to let Sunderland join them in having something to celebrate.

"We had a good rapport with the West Ham lads," says Arnott. "Pop [Robson] had moved backward and forwards between the clubs and afterwards they were as pleased for us getting promotion as we'd been for them to win the cup."

That promotion was signed, sealed and delivered three minutes from time when tiny Stan Cummins wriggled around three defenders before cracking home a shot from outside the box. Cummins was one of two players Sunderland had broken their transfer record to sign during the season and with his 12th goal on his 26th appearance he was looking worth every penny.

The other big money man, Argentinian Claudio Marangoni, had lost his place and was looking like a fish out of water. For another new boy from closer to home the match was his 14th since signing and he'd never been on the losing side. Defender Joe Hinnigan from Wigan had helped secure nine clean sheets as Sunderland finished strongly.

Victory leapfrogged Sunderland from fourth to second. Missing out on goal average were Chelsea, the club who almost 17 years earlier to the day had cruelly ended Sunderland's dreams of a first ever promotion. For Sunderland manager Ken Knighton, assisted by ex Newcastle full back Frank Clark, had done a great job in their first year in charge and the pair soaked up the atmosphere on the lap of honour. It was the perfect way to climax the club's Centenary season. Celebrations continued as Sunderland crossed the Atlantic the following day ahead of a friendly in Miami where they beat Fort Lauderdale Strikers 48 hours after defeating West Ham. That match was a token exhibition game but Sunderland were once again able to bill themselves as a top flight club.

v Liverpool 1-0
Anfield, Division One
May 2nd 1981. Attendance: 40,337

SUNDERLAND	LIVERPOOL	REFEREE
Siddall	Clemence	Mr. C.L. Newsome,
Hinnigan	Neal	Shropshire
Bolton	Money	
Hindmarch	Irwin	
Elliott	Kennedy	
Rowell	Hanson	
Chisholm (Allardyce)	Gayle (Russell)	
Buckley	Lee	
Ritchie	Rush	
Brown	McDermott	
Cummins	Souness	

SEVEN DAYS before this game Sunderland were drawing 1-1 at home to third-bottom Brighton with a minute to go. A point would have done. It would have left the Lads two points better off than the Seagulls and crucially fifteen goals to the good with one game left and still just two points for a win. As the seconds ticked away Brighton defender Gary Williams silenced Roker Park as he scored at the Fulwell End. If anyone had dropped a pin at that moment it would have been heard in all four corners of the ground. The Roker Roar? This was Roker raw. Sunderland had gone from a minute from safety to a long way up a well known creek. Still there was one match left for Sunderland to get the result they'd need to stay up. Where was it again? Oh yes... away to reigning champions Liverpool.

Sunderland's fans have never been anything but top flight. Huge numbers swarmed over Anfield. The 40,000 plus attendance doesn't seem exceptional now but consider this: their previous home gate had been 31,276...against Manchester United. That wasn't the only thing to consider, two other major factors came into play. Firstly Liverpool had a European Cup final against Real Madrid to prepare for and secondly their manager Bob Paisley was a Hetton lad and boyhood Sunderland supporter.

Legend has it that Paisley put a crate of champagne in the Sunderland dressing room before the match. Full back Joe Bolton was playing his 325th – and as it turned out, his last – match for Sunderland. He remembers caretaker manager Mick Docherty coming back from meeting Paisley pre-match when the team sheets were handed in. "We'll be alright lads, just watch the tackles," Bolton reports Docherty as saying.

Evidently Paisley's Liverpool wouldn't be devastated if Sunderland got the result they needed to remain on Liverpool's fixture list the following season. Goalkeeper Barry Siddall admits: "Liverpool weren't at their best and had their final in mind." At one point Bolton got a bit carried away and committed the kind of foul likely to rouse the home side: "There was one there to be won and I went for it, but I just had to calm down and not make any more like that," Joe concedes.

Only the already doomed bottom two and Norwich had lost more than Sunderland away from home and there had only been one away win since September 6th. On the other hand Liverpool had

The Football Echo *heralds the news.*

won 20, drawn seven and lost two of their home league and cup games that season, scoring 77 goals at Anfield in the process.

There didn't look to be much prospect of Liverpool adding to that astonishing tally as the home side rarely threatened and seemed content to play their passing game. Ten years earlier Liverpool had relegated Sunderland at Roker Park with a late goal from full back Chris Lawler. Sunderland's last relegation four years earlier had come on the other side of Stanley Park at Everton but there was no sign of a hat-trick of Merseyside-inflicted misery as the visitors played well, worked like Trojans and then stunned everyone by taking the lead.

Stan Cummins in 2005.

Stan Cummins had wrapped up promotion with his goal against West Ham a year earlier and he helped Sunderland take a stride to safety with another terrific shot here after he collected the ball from Gary Rowell. "The goal Stan Cummins scored that day was right in the corner. There's no way their keeper would have stopped that. No keeper would – not even Monty would have stopped it," Bolton points out. Cummins was the only ever present in the side and this 10th goal of the season was just reward for the contribution he made. He was always a popular player and this was one of his great moments.

As so often has been the case, Sunderland's crucial goal in a big game arrived just after the half hour mark, 32 minutes to be precise. It meant there was an awfully long time to hang on but Liverpool failed to apply any sustained pressure and an unlikely first win at

Anfield in 20 years, and first in the top flight since Sunderland's title winning season of 1935/36, was achieved.

There was just one notable scare when Seaton Delaval-born Ray Kennedy hit the bar with a shot from distance. Had he scored perhaps it would have gone down well with Magpie mates from home and it might have offered Kennedy a little revenge for being in the Arsenal side that lost to Sunderland in the FA Cup semi-final eight years before. The luck was with Sunderland though and Siddall had little trouble in keeping his fifth clean sheet since returning to the team in February.

The final whistle of a famous victory was welcomed with rapture but as the other results came through it transpired that even if Sunderland had lost they would have stayed up. Norwich were the unfortunate team to join Leicester and Palace in going down, Sunderland managing to finish sixth off bottom.

For caretaker boss Docherty and centre half Sam Allardyce it was the end of the road with Sunderland as it was for stalwart cult hero Bolton. New manager Alan Durban would arrive in the summer although in a year's time Sunderland would again be looking for a result to stay up.

It wasn't the first time Sunderland had beaten a side about to play a European Cup final in their final trip of the season – Manchester United had lost to the Lads in 1968. However Sunderland supporters willed the Merseysiders on that little bit extra come May 27th when they faced Real Madrid in Paris. Liverpool won that match 1-0... with a goal from Sunderland-born Alan Kennedy.

Walk on, walk on with hope in your hearts, and you'll never walk alone.

v Manchester Utd 3-2

Roker Park, Division One
November 24th 1984. Attendance: 25,405

SUNDERLAND	MANCHESTER UTD	REFEREE
Turner	Bailey	Mr. J. Key,
Venison	Gidman	Rotherham
Daniel	Duxbury	
Bennett	Garton	
Chisholm	McQueen	
Berry	Strachan	
Hodgson	Moses	
Gayle	Robson	
West	Olsen (Muhren)	
Cummins	Hughes	
Walker (Lemon)	Whiteside	

THIS WASN'T so much of a 'Greatest Game' as a 'greatest first half'. Five goals, two penalties, a hat-trick and two sendings-off all took place before half-time. Certainly there have been other notable first periods such as twice being 6-1 up (v Fairfield 1895 and Rotherham 1987) 7-0 down (v 'Sheffield' Wednesday 1911), Cliff Whitelum scoring five in a wartime cup final or Davie Halliday four in a 4-2 scoreline in 1928, but for sheer drama the first 45 minutes of this meeting with Manchester United was unforgettable.

Sunderland were two down within quarter of an hour as United turned on the style and scored twice in three minutes. Bryan Robson netted from a rebound from his own initial shot in the 13th minute and before Sunderland could recover the visitors doubled their lead when Mark Hughes received from Norman Whiteside and slipped the ball past Chris Turner. Two year earlier Hughes and Whiteside had been magnificent at Roker in the FA Youth Cup semi-final and they looked like tearing Sunderland apart again.

Sunderland though got straight back into the game with a brilliant shot from left winger Clive Walker. Two minutes later the game boiled over when Hughes and Sunderland's Dave Hodgson

Howard Gayle distracts the Man United defence.

squared up to each other on the halfway line and were promptly dismissed by referee Key.

With over seventy minutes to go an already open game suddenly had even more space to exploit. Mid-table Sunderland and second-from-top United went at it hammer and tongs with plenty of goalmouth action.

There were no further goals until five minutes before half-time but then for the second time in the game there were two goals in two minutes and this time both came from penalties for Sunderland. Centre back Gary Bennett was renowned for storming forward – in years to come he'd score a last-minute winner against United from such a run. On that occasion as this Gary Bailey was the United keeper who on this over-heated day had a rush of blood to the head and dashed out to bring Benno down.

Centre forward Colin West was the normal penalty taker but Walker grabbed the ball, full of confidence after already scoring. Walker slotted the ball past Bailey to equalise and within two minutes repeated the feat to complete his hat-trick after giant defender

That evening's Football Echo.

Gary Bailey punches clear of Gary Bennett
as Gordon Chisholm and Gordon McQueen look on.

Gordon McQueen cleaned out 5'4" Stan Cummins, who was torturing the visiting defenders with his close control and twisting, darting runs.

United had won their last four games but they could be vulnerable. A month earlier they'd leaked five at Everton and they were on the ropes and hanging on for some half-time respite as West and Cummins brought saves out of Bailey in the final couple of minutes of what had been a sensational first half.

A week short of a decade earlier the same clubs had provided a 3-2 scoreline and 'Match of the Season' fare for the BBC and while the second half was something of a case of 'After the Lord Mayor's Show' it was still enthralling entertainment for that night's *Match of the Day* with the BBC at Roker.

Sunderland were good value for the victory and continued to take the game to United in the second half with Turner never seriously tested in the visitors' quest for an equaliser. The best chance of the second half fell to Howard Gayle five minutes from time only for the ex Liverpool man to hurry his shot.

The damage though had been done and Walker would score again in the return fixture late in the season when the Lads shared the points from a 2-2 draw at Old Trafford: "The highlight of my time with Sunderland was scoring a hat-trick against Manchester United," says Walker. "That was one of the highlights of my whole career and I also scored at Old Trafford that season. There's not many players can claim to have scored four times against Man United in one season."

It was Sunderland's fourth home successive league win and the third in a row where they'd scored three goals. The points took Sunderland to 11th in the 22-strong league but dismal late season form after the Milk (League) Cup final, when Walker missed a penalty, resulted in relegation. "We went down that season but I was proud to be top scorer from the wing because at least I'd done all I could to try and prevent relegation," says the Londoner. "If only we'd had another midfielder or forward contributing that number of goals, we'd probably have stayed up."

v Tottenham H 2-1

White Hart Lane, League (Milk) Cup
fourth round replay. December 5th
1984. Attendance: 25,835

SUNDERLAND	TOTTENHAM H	REFEREE
Turner	Clemence	Mr. B. Stevens,
Venison	Stevens	Gloucestershire
Daniel	Hughton	
Bennett	Roberts	
Chisholm	Miller	
Elliott	Perryman	
Berry	Chiedozie	
Gayle	Falco	
Hodgson (West)	Allen (Mabbutt)	
Proctor	Hoddle	
Walker	Hazard	

SUNDERLAND HAVE a long tradition of great goalkeepers. This cup tie showed one of them at his very best; Chris Turner's performance against Spurs and indeed throughout this entire cup run was the biggest single factor in taking Sunderland to Wembley.

Turner had already played a blinder in keeping Spurs at bay in the original tie at Roker which had finished goalless a fortnight earlier. Now that they had home advantage, Spurs were confident of progressing especially as they'd had the better of the match at Roker Park.

Two of the Tottenham team, Clive Allen and Graham Roberts, had been sent off at Sunderland in the league earlier in the season when Spurs had lost to a penalty and there was a feeling that they owed the north easterners. Roberts didn't have long to wait to put Sunderland 'in their place'. Just five minutes had gone when Spurs were given a penalty for a foul by Gordon Chisholm. Roberts emphatically thumped it home to put Spurs ahead.

Peter Shreeves' Spurs had knocked Liverpool out in the previous round and were the UEFA Cup holders, all in all a talented team. England international Glenn Hoddle was their star man and he was

ably supported by Sun-
derland-born Mickey Hazard.
The pair enjoyed spraying the
ball around White Hart Lane
and in John Chiedozie they
had a speed merchant on the
wing who was capable of
burning off the quickest of
defenders. With a powerful

Barry Venison

target man in Mark Falco, partnered with a deadly finisher in the
shape of Allen, Spurs were an excellent team who would finish third
in the table whereas Sunderland would fall away and end up
relegated. On this occasion though, the Wearsiders produced a
tremendous performance to surprise Spurs and perhaps even
themselves.

Marshalled by Shaun Elliott, Sunderland didn't cave in and
gradually began to find a foothold in the game despite their bad start.

Chris Turner

Mid-way through the first half
they got back on level terms.
Former Liverpool men David
Hodgson and Howard Gayle
linked well to create a chance
for Clive Walker who gave
another ex Liverpool man,
goalkeeper Ray Clemence, no
chance.

With Turner on top of his
game and supremely confident,
Tottenham were getting no joy
from their frequent attacks and
had to guard against Sunderland who were looking dangerous on the break with Gayle
blowing hot and Bennett

always ready to shrink the yards with his long stride while Walker had the beating of Stevens.

Sunderland were good value for the one all score-line going in at half-time and immediately shocked Spurs straight after the break by going ahead. This time Gordon Chisholm got the goal, atoning for conceding the earlier penalty. 'Chis' enjoyed a stroke of good fortune, his shot leaving Clemence wrong-footed after striking defender Paul Miller.

Gordon Chisholm

Stung, Spurs came forward in wave after wave of attacks but Turner took everything in his stride and spread confidence to those in front of him. As time wore on the home crowd became more and more frustrated and the home players more and more frantic in their efforts to get the ball forward.

Eventually something had to give and with ten minutes to go the referee awarded Tottenham their second penalty of the evening after skipper Elliott was adjudged to have handled a Chris Hughton cross. Roberts blasted his penalty towards the bottom corner and was beginning to acclaim his 'goal' only for Turner to somehow get there and push the drilled shot away. It was a marvellous save and gave Spurs the same 'thou shalt not pass' message that Monty gave to Leeds at Wembley on the last occasion Sunderland reached a cup final.

Len Ashurst's team still had a lot of work to do to get to that final but having knocked out Spurs Sunderland saw no reason why they couldn't go further. Watford were beaten away in the fifth round and Chelsea dramatically overcome by a comprehensive aggregate 5-2 semi-final score-line, Sunderland winning both legs. At Wembley against Norwich in what became known as the 'Friendly

Len Ashurst

Final' Sunderland went down by a single deflected goal in a match where it was their turn to miss a penalty.

The season ended disastrously with the drop doubling up with a poor cup final showing but on this night at White Hart Lane, Sunderland and Chris Turner in particular, were superb. Spurs had eight home cup ties that season, losing twice, to Sunderland and Real Madrid. The Lads were in good company but the quality shown in this match was sadly to prove the exception rather than the rule.

v Stoke City 2-0

Roker Park, Division Two
May 3rd 1986. Attendance: 20,631

SUNDERLAND	STOKE CITY	REFEREE
Dibble	Fox	Mr. D. Hutchinson,
Venison	Callaghan (Painter)	Harrogate
Kennedy	Hemming	
Gray	Mills	
Bennett	Bould	
Elliott	Berry	
Ford	Adams	
Gayle	Saunders	
Wallace	Bertschin	
Gates	Shaw	
Proctor (Hodgson)	Heath	

WHEN CHAIRMAN Tom Cowie appointed the big name manager supporters craved before the start of the season, appetites were whetted that there would be some big games to look forward to. This last-day-of-the-season nail-biter where a win was required to avoid the possibility of a first ever demotion to the third division was definitely not what people had in mind when Lawrie McMenemy took over.

McMenemy was a larger than life character with a huge media profile. He'd enjoyed success at Southampton, most notably guiding them to an FA Cup final win as a second division club over Manchester United three years after Bob Stokoe had performed his miracle at Sunderland. Most supporters believed McMenemy was an unmitigated disaster at Roker however and when he eventually did a midnight flit, departing in the dead of night, not even Stokoe could save Sunderland. It would be 11 months from this date that McMenemy left, leaving Sunderland destined to drop into the third division for the first (and to date only) time in history.

Sunderland's only full season under McMenemy began with five defeats and not a goal scored. Trying to re-create his Southampton policy of signing big name players in the twilight of their careers, his line-up v Stoke included former England international Eric Gates, ex Liverpool and England man Alan Kennedy and former Forest and Scotland man Frank Gray, the latter two having European Cup winners' medals to their names. Scottish international George Burley had played for the reserves that week and, along with ex Crystal Palace centre forward Dave Swindlehurst, was out of the side.

Lawrie McMenemy

It was in goal that Sunderland had had their biggest headaches. Following relegation from the top flight the previous season, Chris Turner had been sold for a joint record fee to Manchester United. In his place McMenemy had signed Seamus McDonagh, a keeper who infamously complained the goals were the wrong size at Grimsby. He was soon replaced by Bob Bolder, once of Liverpool, but it wasn't until 20-year-old Andy 'Officer' Dibble was signed on loan from Luton for the last couple of the months of the season that the fans felt they had confidence in their last line of defence.

On the penultimate Saturday of the season the long trip home from a 3-1 defeat at Brighton was made in the knowledge that two wins were needed from the last two games, or else Sunderland could plummet from the top flight to the third division in just 12 months. Dibble had excelled in keeping a midweek clean sheet as lowly Shrewsbury were beaten at home and now a repeat was needed against Stoke.

Tension was the order of the day as over 20,000 nervous souls made their way to Roker Park. This was the 100th league meeting of the clubs and good games between Sunderland and Stoke were as rare as post-war trophies but no one was interested in seeing a good game – they just wanted a win, however it was managed.

Sunderland got off to the perfect start, taking the lead in the second minute. Gates darted into the box and was brought down by his old Ipswich teammate Mick Mills, now player/manager of the visitors. Mark Proctor stepped up to beat Peter Fox. There were only 88 minutes to hang on.

Fulham were already down but only three points separated Sunderland, Boro, Carlisle, Blackburn and Shrewsbury with two of the five destined for the drop, Shrewsbury and Boro playing each other with the other two rivals at home, Carlisle against promotion chasing Charlton although they also had one more game at Oldham two days later.

Following Proctor's penalty, play was scrappy as Sunderland remained

Mark Proctor

on edge while Stoke produced 'route one' football putting the home back four under pressure. Shaun Elliott was one of Sunderland's best players but nerves even got the better of him as he almost gifted Stoke an equaliser with an underhit back pass that Dibble had to be very alert to, otherwise Graham Shaw would have equalised.

Howard Gayle was proving to be Sunderland's most potent attacking outlet, his pace causing problems but there was no end product and Sunderland were unable to establish the two goal cushion that could have calmed them. Proctor was at the heart of most of Sunderland's good work, at one point combining with veterans Gates and Gray for the latter to test Fox.

Sensing Sunderland's anxiety Stoke began to apply more and more pressure not least through Keith Bertschin. He had a habit of scoring against the Lads and had netted the winner in the reverse fixture earlier in the season. Just over a year later he'd sign for Sunderland and two decades later return as reserve team coach.

Fortunately, as the visitors were getting on top and asking questions of the home defence, Sunderland got a second goal with a helping hand from another man who would later come to Sunderland. Steve Bould played a key role in helping Sunderland settle in the top flight after their first promotion since moving to the Stadium of Light. By then he was a big name after a great career with Arsenal but in May 1986 he was an up-and-coming 23-year-old with his home town club and from a free kick he conceded for a foul on Gayle, Sunderland scored their second.

The goal brought a release to the tension that enveloped the stadium. 68 minutes had gone when Proctor laid the dead ball off to Gray who cracked in a fierce shot that beat Fox all ends up. Tails now up, Sunderland suddenly looked a different team, confidence replacing anxiety as full back Kennedy stormed forward to shoot just wide while Ian Wallace, Gary Bennett and Gates all fired in efforts in the closing stages.

Nonetheless there was evidence of an unhappy camp by the angry reaction of Gayle when he was brought off but as the final whistle sounded on a dreadful season, with Sunderland safe while Boro and Carlisle fell through the relegation trapdoor, it looked as if the worst part was over. Surely McMenemy would learn and Sunderland would push for promotion next year. They would get out of the second division... but not as planned.

v Gillingham 4-3

Aggregate 6-6 after extra time.
Roker Park, Division Two and Three, play-off semi-final, second leg. May 17th 1987
Attendance: 25,470

SUNDERLAND	GILLINGHAM	REFEREE
Hesford	Kite	Referee: Mr. M. Peck,
Lemon	Haylock	Kendal
Kennedy (Corner)	Pearce	
Doyle	Berry	
Gray	Quow	
Bennett	Greenhall	
Armstrong	Pritchard	
Proctor	Weatherley (Shearer)	
Bertschin	Smith	
Swindlehurst	Elsey	
Gates	Cascarino	

INTERVIEWED ON the Wembley turf ahead of Coventry's FA Cup final with Spurs, Nick Pickering's mind should have been fully focussed on the cup final. It wasn't: "Best of luck to Sunderland tomorrow" was his message. Sunderland weren't playing at Wembley where Pickering had played for the Lads two years before in the League Cup final. Instead they were preparing for a play-off match with Gillingham. Pickering had been one of two England U21 international full backs Sunderland could have built a team around, but had been sold along with Barry Venison by manager Lawrie McMenemy who preferred to bring in veterans who had tasted cup finals rather than relegation play-offs.

"Alan Kennedy and George Burley found it hard," says Gary Bennett who captained Sunderland at the time. "Those two had played in and won European finals and suddenly they were in a play-off to decide whether or not we went down into the third division. It was a different type of big game to what they were used to and a different type of football and a different type of pressure."

There was pressure alright. McMenemy had resigned after a desperate home defeat by Sheffield United left Sunderland perilously close to the bottom having taken one point from six games. Never before had Sunderland been in the third division although they'd come very close the year before. McMenemy jumped ship – like the *Titanic* he should never have left Southampton.

New Sunderland chairman Bob Murray turned to cup winning legend Bob Stokoe to guide the club who had a ship on their badge through the icebergs and to safety. He might as well have sent for Captain Bligh.

Sunderland slumped into the play-offs. These were being contested for the first time since Victorian times when they were called 'Test Matches'. In 1897 Sunderland had survived this ordeal and gone on to become the last club to lose the claim to have been the only team never to have played outside the top flight when they were relegated for the first time in 1958. Sunderland now found themselves in a play-off to stop them losing the full membership they'd had of the Football League since 1890 and sinking to the level of 'Associate Member'.

On the final day of the regular season Sunderland missed a crucial penalty and lost 3-2 to Barnsley. The result dropped Sunderland into the bottom three and therefore into the play-offs. The idea was that the third-bottom team in division two would play the fifth-top side from the third division with the winners meeting the winners of a play-off between the teams finishing third and fourth in division three for a place in the second division. Games were over two legs and away goals would count double.

Gillingham won the Thursday night first leg 3-2 at their Priestfield Stadium where the 13,804 gate was almost three times their average. Three days later the Sunderland team showed two changes from the first leg. Missing were centre half Steve Hetzke who'd been injured and young defender David Corner who dropped to the bench. In came Paul 'Jack' Lemon at right back – only the second time he'd played there – and Eric Gates, who had come on as sub at Gillingham.

Within three minutes Sunderland had let in a goal, meaning they were 4-2 down on aggregate. It was the only one of Gillingham's six goals over the two legs not scored by Tony Cascarino, this time Howard Pritchard being the henchman.

Sunderland needed inspiration and it came from little Eric Gates, the former England international from Ferryhill. Two goals from him in the 17th and 22nd minutes had Sunderland all square and in fact if there was no further scoring the red and whites would win on away goals.

Eleven minutes later came the key moment: a penalty to Sunderland that was missed. Mark Proctor had missed from the spot against Barnsley but his two goals at Gillingham had included a penalty. Clive Walker and Michael Gray at Wembley in 1985 and 1998? This penalty miss proved to be even more of a disaster. Had it gone in the chances are Sunderland would have never suffered the ignominy of division three football. Keeper Kite saved with his legs and the wind drained out of Sunderland.

The Lads had been denied blatant penalties for fouls on Bennett and Bertschin before the referee finally gave one for handball on the line but early in the second half it was the Gills' turn to be given an opportunity from the spot after keeper Iain Hesford felled goalscorer Pritchard seven minutes after half-time. Hesford got to Colin Greenall's penalty but that man Cascarino turned the ball in when Trevor Quow blasted the ball back into the danger area.

For over half an hour Sunderland scrambled for a goal as they trailed 5-4 on aggregate. Gillingham always seemed to get a body in the way and as the minutes raced by the colour drained out of supporters' faces as the prospect of third division football loomed.

"I swapped positions with Dave Swindlehurst," says Gary Bennett who was playing despite injury. "Swinders went back to play centre half and I went up front and managed to score the goal to send us into extra time. A cross came in and I managed to get my head to it. Everything just fell into place, there was uproar when it hit the net." Uproar is an understatement. Roker had seen great games before, league titles, promotion clinchers, big cup ties, even relegations, but never a play-off and never with such a low ebb in the club's history at stake. The captain had scored a goal any captain would be proud of but *A Question of Sport* might enquire 'What Happened Next?'

"The 90 minutes were up almost straight after my goal," explains Benno. "The aggregate score was 5-5, each team having won 3-2 on their home ground. The play-offs were new to everybody, no-one was familiar with them and we didn't know what was happening. I remember going into it [extra time] thinking, 'Do away goals count?'... there was extra time to think about and would away goals count then?... we thought, 'Is it going to penalties or what?' "

Iain Hesford

Yes away goals did count in extra time and Gillingham soon had one, Cascarino three minutes in. Sunderland needed to score two more and while Keith Bertschin scored with a superb diving header to make it 4-3 to Sunderland and 6-6 overall it wasn't enough.

Sunderland duly became the only team in history to be relegated on the away goals rule – despite identical scorelines over 90 minutes on each ground. Relegated then because the extra time which you drew was on your ground! The Football League swiftly changed the rules but it was too late; the third division was the division Sunderland were in and really they had no one to blame but themselves. The extra time was at the end of the 44th league and play-off game of the season, there had been plenty of time to do something about their situation.

In the Clock Stand a few hundred Newcastle supporters celebrated Sunderland's relegation. It was May 17th 1987. One day short of three years later the sweetest revenge would be taken in another play-off game. This was the worst of times, but the best of times was to come.

v **Newcastle Utd** 2-0

St. James' Park. Play-off semi-final
second leg. Aggregate score 0-2
May 16th 1990. Attendance: 31,199

SUNDERLAND	NEWCASTLE UTD	REFEREE
Norman	Burridge	Mr. G.Courtney,
Kay	Scott	Spennymoor
Agboola	Stimson	
Bennett	Aitken	
MacPhail	Anderson	
Owers	Bradshaw (Dillon)	
Bracewell	Brock	
Armstrong	Askew (O'Brien)	
Gates	Quinn	
Gabbiadini	McGhee	
Hawke	Kristensen	
Unused subs: Brady,		
Hauser		

THERE'S NO such thing as an unimportant derby. Perhaps only the one at St. James' in 1903 that stopped Sunderland retaining the championship compares with this one for magnitude, although had Sunderland not lost the 1955 FA Cup semi-final to Manchester City, a cup final against the Magpies (who'd won a semi-final replay against York at Roker Park) at Wembley would have taken some beating. Tony Norman who played in goal for Sunderland in this game doesn't agree. He says: "People come up to me and say 'Wasn't it great when you beat Newcastle?' and I say, 'It was for nothing. What did we get?'" Norman's view is that as that was the semi-final and Sunderland lost the final to Swindon it was worthless. Notwithstanding the fact that Sunderland won promotion after Swindon were punished for financial irregularities, for every Sunderland supporter a win over the Magpies is one to savour but to beat them in their own back yard in a play-off game was extra special with cream on top.

With the first leg goalless at Roker Park, having ended in controversy when Sunderland's Paul Hardyman was sent off in the last minute for kicking Newcastle goalie John Burridge in the follow up to his own saved penalty, Newcastle thought all they had to do was turn up for the second leg and they'd win. Of course Sunderland people have heard ad infinitum about what Newcastle are going to do – that's what makes stopping them so amusing to Wearsiders.

"They were full of it and I'm sure they thought they'd done the job," says Marco Gabbiadini of the Newcastle team's reaction in the tunnel after the first leg. Gabbiadini had been brought down for the penalty and it would be his goal that would finish them off in the second leg. "As we walked to the dressing room after the first leg the Newcastle team were walking down one end of the tunnel and we were walking down the other – and they're screaming, 'Yes!' and sound ecstatic with the result," says Tony Norman, adding: "This to me was music to my ears. I loved it...from the moment I heard them cheer I thought, 'this is perfect, St. James' Park here we go' because they thought they'd already done the hard part."

Most Sunderland supporters felt the same. Newcastle had finished above the Lads in the table but Sunderland had been the better team in all three drawn derbies. Moreover Sunderland's away form was red hot, six of the last seven had been won and apart from the solitary third division season you had to go back to 1923/24 to find a season where Sunderland had won so many away games.

Newcastle's Mark McGhee hit the outside of the post in the first few minutes, not that Tony Norman was even slightly perturbed: "I know this sounds funny," he says, "but when he hit it I thought, 'that's not in'. Sometimes when you're playing and you're on top of everything, the ball travels in slow motion and you have so much time to react."

It didn't take Sunderland long to take the lead. From a John Kay throw, Gabbiadini played the ball to Gary Owers – a man so red and white that years later when he was manager of Forest Green Rovers, who play in black and white stripes, he made them play in their away kit in a friendly against Sunderland. He got to the goal line and squared for Gates to apply the finishing touch. It had taken 13 minutes to let the air out of Tyneside's over-inflated balloon.

The Sunderland supporters were in the old Leazes End. At the back of the opposite Gallowgate End was a scoreboard with the descending time in yellow letters. The away fans counted those minutes down with little in the way of the tension that might have been expected. The fans knew Sunderland were the better team and there was a little touch of the old '73 cup run confidence.

Sunderland were largely in control. The G-Force of Gates and Gabbiadini were always likely to get another goal, Newcastle were only mounting sporadic attacks and we now know that in any case Tony Norman was seeing the ball come to him as if it was in slow motion. It wasn't just the ball, Newcastle seemed to be in slow motion, Sunderland were quicker in thought and deed.

Owers had a chance in the 69th minute, Newcastle needing a last-ditch tackle from Mark Stimson to survive but then with four minutes on the clock and Sunderland looking comfortable the G-Force did what they'd been doing for the last three seasons. The move started with youngster Warren Hawke – in the side due to Hardyman's suspension – bringing Gabbiadini into play. Marco takes up the

Marco makes it 2-0.

story: "Eric was a master, whenever I got that split second to look up, he would always be available. I went past one and he came off his markers a yard, so I played it for him. He'd always put it into space for me to run onto. He did so this time, but I was wider than I thought and on my weaker side...I caught it nice, didn't blast it. I knew Burridge couldn't get near it. I was only about nine or ten yards from the touchline, but the angle was a good fifteen yards across goal. It seemed to take an age to go in." Evidently Marco, like his keeper, was seeing things in 'slo-mo'. "I remember wheeling away thinking, 'Is it going in or what?' There was just that split second as I was turning away to celebrate when I thought it might hit the post. It was a perfect goal though."

It certainly was and what was more it was 2-0 with four minutes left. Twenty minutes later it was still 2-0 and the game was still being played. For 19 of those minutes the teams had been taking shelter in the tunnel and dressing rooms as the Newcastle fans had invaded the pitch – as they'd done when 3-1 down to Nottingham Forest in 1974. On that occasion the match was abandoned, Newcastle won a replay on a neutral ground and eventually made it to Wembley. It was Sunderland going to Wembley this time though because Spenny-moor-based referee George Courtney made it clear to the players that no matter how long it took and even if he had to have the ground cleared they'd be going out to finish the final four minutes that night.

"I saw those like another game," explains the Norman who refused to be conquered, "I didn't care if there were four minutes or another twenty. I looked at it as a third match, which I needed to keep a clean sheet in. That's the way I concentrated. Looking at the Newcastle players, you could see that their heart had gone."

When the players emerged those last four minutes were played in an eerie atmosphere. Newcastle's fans had given up the ghost, and many had left the stadium. Sunderland's fans were delirious but knew there'd be a welcoming party for them outside and that they had to get back to Wearside alive. There were tickets for Wembley to queue for after all.

v Manchester City 2-3

Maine Road, Division One
May 11th 1991. Attendance: 39,194

SUNDERLAND	MANCHESTER CITY	REFEREE
Norman	Margetson	Mr. A. Gunn,
Owers	Hill	South Chailey,
Hardyman (Hauser)	Pointon	Sussex
Bennett	Heath	
Ord	Hendry	
Pascoe	Redmond	
Bracewell	White	
Hawke (Brady)	Brennan	
Davenport	Quinn	
Gabbiadini	Harper	
Kay	Clarke (Beckford)	
	Unused sub: Ward	

SUNDERLAND WENT into this final game of the season at Maine Road with their top flight survival hanging by a thread. They could win and still go down or lose and still stay up. Only two teams went down and Sunderland were second-bottom. However they were level on points and goal difference with Luton Town although Luton had scored four more so the Lads would need to better whatever the Hatters achieved in their game. Unfortunately their final fixture was at home to already-relegated Derby.

Sunderland were away to fifth-placed Manchester City. They had no chance of European qualification but the incentive of trying to finish above Manchester United was the target of player-manager Peter Reid. He had taken over as manager from Howard Kendall shortly after City's draw at Sunderland in November. There was to be no old pals act from Reid to Sunderland captain Paul Bracewell, the pair having been central midfield partners in Everton's great side of the mid-eighties.

Reid of course would be a successful Sunderland manager before the end of the decade and his move to Wearside would result in two of City's team also coming to join the Lads: Adrian Heath and Niall Quinn. It would be Quinn who would score twice to send Sunderland down but in fact because of the outcome of the Luton v Derby game Sunderland would have had to win by three goals to have avoided the drop.

If there's one thing you can count on when it comes to Sunderland though it is that no matter what the odds there'll always be that little glimmer of hope that the Lads might just pull it off. Even without the suspended Kevin Ball Sunderland put up a fighting display refusing to bow even after Quinn gave the home side a 10th-minute lead.

Richard Ord and City's Colin Hendry.

Sunderland had nothing to lose by going for it so attacked City at every opportunity. Just before half-time the goals flowed. Top scorer Gabbiadini got the equaliser in the 40th minute, thumping home a header from a John Kay cross. Four minutes later the Lads went ahead through Gary Bennett who had started his career with City. Excitement maybe got the better of the players as well as the fans because having turned the game round in four minutes, concentration levels slipped and the minute there was to go to the break was all it took Niall Quinn to draw City level.

"We had to get a result against Man City," remembers Bennett. "Niall Quinn played up front for City in that game. He scored two and was a real handful. He was a good player...we thought we could go and get a result but we never do anything the easy way at Sunderland."

John Kay

Ears tuned to radios brought bad half-time information with the news that Luton were a goal up. Frustratingly it was an own goal scored by Sunderland-born (and future Sunderland player) Mick Harford, who had scored an O.G. shortly before half-time to put his former club Luton ahead. Worse news was to follow when Lars Elstrup doubled Luton's lead two minutes into the second half. If there was no further change to the scoreline at Kenilworth Road, Sunderland would need to win 5-2 to stay up.

In fact the match at Maine Road continued to be an open attacking one but there was never any chance of Sunderland beating a top side by three clear goals. German centre forward Thomas Hauser and enigmatic winger Kieron Brady (who'd scored against City keeper Margetson for the reserves two weeks earlier) were thrown into the fray but the only further goal came in the last minute from City's David White to condemn Sunderland to defeat as well as demotion.

It was all over bar the shouting – but there was plenty of that still going on. Sunderland's away support is massive but this was one of the biggest turn outs for a league game and a relegation game at that. Around 14,000 Sunderland supporters gave City their biggest gate of the season. It was almost three thousand more than they'd had for their derby with Man Utd which was their second highest gate and over 15,000 more than City had had for their previous home league game. Sunderland supporters packed the Platt Lane Stand and also took over a substantial part of the giant Kippax terracing that ran along the side of Maine Road.

Sunderland though had been relegated just one season after promotion. Gallingly for the red and white army, Luton, who had stayed up, had a crowd of just 12,889 for their do-or-die decider. It was their biggest gate of the season and represented fewer fans at home than Sunderland had taken away. However it's long been realised that if you got points for supporters Sunderland would be Champions League quality. Nonetheless it was that sort of phenomenal support that left a mark on Messrs Reid and Quinn, both of whom came north in later years to try and give those fans something to cheer about.

v Chelsea 2-1

Roker Park, FA Cup quarter-final replay
March 18th 1992. Attendance: 26,039

SUNDERLAND	CHELSEA	REFEREE
Norman	Beasant	Mr. T. Holbrook,
Kay	Clarke	Weightwick,
Rogan	Cundy (Allen)	West Midlands
Ball	Elliott	
Hardyman (Ord)	Sinclair	
Rush	Wise	
Bracewell	Townsend	
Atkinson	Jones	
Armstrong	Le Saux (Stuart)	
Davenport	Dixon	
Byrne	Cascarino	
Unused sub: Brady		

WHEN SUNDERLAND reached the FA Cup final in 1992 this was undoubtedly the best game of the cup run. Although Roker Park didn't close for another five years it was also the last time Sunderland ever won an FA Cup tie there. It was fully in keeping with the cup tradition that in this last great Roker cup tie the manager of the visiting team was none other than the hero of 1973: Ian Porterfield.

In contrast, in charge of Sunderland was caretaker manager Malcolm Crosby, who had taken over five days before the FA Cup 3rd round. Sunderland had reached the quarter-final and had earned a replay with a terrific 1-1 draw at Stamford Bridge played on a Monday night for the benefit of live TV. Chelsea's goal that night had come from an erroneously awarded corner kick with second division Sunderland feeling they had done enough to win.

Supporters clamoured for more cup glory but police instructions regarding segregation and the return of some tickets from the visitors meant that the sold out signs were up despite the ground being under capacity. No doubt the authorities were mindful of the crowd trouble at both legs of the League (Milk) Cup semi-final between the clubs seven years earlier. Right from the kick-off the match was a cracker. Sunderland were missing two of their best players, Bennett and Owers, through injury and had had four players including goalkeeper Tony Norman and defender Paul Hardyman receiving treatment until just before the game; indeed Hardyman was unable to continue after half-time but the introduction of the taller Richard Ord served Sunderland well as the longer the game went on the more the Londoners resorted to high balls.

Tony Norman

Sunderland hit the ground running as they attacked the Fulwell End and the early pressure drew first blood when Peter Davenport scored his first goal in over two months. The move began with two of Sunderland's young local lads, Brian Atkinson winning the ball and playing in David Rush on the right wing. Rush was aptly named and had pace to burn, something that caused Chelsea problems all night. John Byrne was no slouch either and when he received Rush's pass he glided past defender Paul Elliott as if he wasn't there and got in his shot. Former Newcastle keeper Dave Beasant couldn't hold it and as the ball ran loose former England man Davenport was there to accept the tap-in.

Davenport had a chance to double the lead soon after but fired over the bar. It would have been a second goal the Lads could have done with. Before half-time Chelsea began to get to grips with the wind and had largely drawn Sunderland's sting. Chelsea were unbeaten in six away trips since the turn of the year, a run that included games at Old Trafford and Anfield and they came back confidently. Norman had to dash out of his box to head clear when striker Kerry Dixon burst clear and moments later the keeper was forced to produce the first of several spectacular saves he would make to deny Dixon again. Just on half-time Dixon then fluffed his lines, missing a sitter, but as the teams went in at half-time Sunderland knew it was going to take a Herculean effort to keep Chelsea at bay.

Tony Norman had many great games for Sunderland. Two years earlier he'd been brilliant at Wembley in the play-off final and to help get Sunderland into this tie with Chelsea he'd produced one of the all time great saves to deny West Ham's Tim Breacker. Once again Tony was in top form here and he needed to be. Soon after the restart he had Dixon cursing him again and then just short of the hour mark he somehow stopped a point blank header from Dennis Wise. "I stood up and it came straight at me," says Norman. "Again, right place, right time. That was an important save and for a long time it looked like we might just hang on and win 1-0."

Sunderland needed to ease the pressure and pushed hard for the second goal, Davenport testing Beasant three minutes after Norman's wonder save. Once again Beasant could only parry but though Davenport got to the rebound first Elliott was able to hack his second effort away from just short of the line. Soon afterwards Byrne found the back of the net only for an offside flag to cut short the cheers.

Dixon had had no luck against Norman but lurking alongside him as twin striker was a man who knew all about scoring against Sunderland: Tony Cascarino, scourge of the play-offs five years earlier when he'd scored five times for Gillingham. He'd been quiet but with 14 minutes to go his head rose highest to head a free kick from Wise goalwards. He'd used up his luck against Sunderland though and this time the crossbar came to the rescue. As Chelsea cranked up the pressure an equaliser looked inevitable, twice captain Paul Bracewell cleared off the line but finally the resistance was broken. There were just five minutes left when two of football's 'pantomime villains' combined to bring the tie level, Vinnie Jones knocking the ball on for Wise to finally beat Norman with a neat close-range flick.

Sunderland had given everything and then some. They were out on their feet while Chelsea looked stronger and had dominated the closing stages. It looked as if extra time would be a formality for the visitors, the cup run would be at an end and the harsh reality of life in the bottom half of Division Two would be all there was left of the season.

David Rush had the lungs and the legs for one last dash at the Londoners and forced a corner at the Roker End on the Clock Stand side. Brian Atkinson kept it away from the keeper with an outswinger to almost the edge of the box. Coming in to meet it with all the power of a Charlie Hurley was Gordon Armstrong. He could not possibly have made better contact with his header and as it thumped into the back of the net everyone present instantly knew they had just witnessed one of the great cup goals. It was one of those 'I was there' moments. Chelsea were finished. They'd given it everything to get an equaliser but within moments they were behind again with just three minutes to go.

Armstrong had scored an almost identical goal in the first week of the season in a midweek match at Barnsley but as Jimmy Montgomery could tell him, if you come up with a magical moment in the FA Cup it will never be forgotten. Sure enough, Gordon's goal is up there with Monty's double save but Tony Norman's contribution to a great cup win should not be forgotten either.

"If somebody said to me now, 'you played over 700 games over 21 years, what was the best atmosphere?' I'd say that Chelsea game. Without a doubt," says Tony Norman. "It just had something on the night, better than Wembley even."

v Liverpool 0-2

Wembley, FA Cup final
May 9th 1992. Attendance: 79,544

SUNDERLAND	LIVERPOOL	REFEREE
Norman	Grobbelaar	Mr. P. Don,
Owers	Jones	Middlesex
Rogan	Burrows	
Ball	Nicol	
Bennett	Molby	
Rush (Hardyman)	Wright	
Bracewell	Saunders	
Atkinson (Hawke)	Houghton	
Armstrong	Rush	
Byrne	McManaman	
Davenport	Thomas	
	Unused subs: Marsh,	
	Walters	

SUNDERLAND'S FOURTH FA Cup final and second as a second division side pitted them against Liverpool. The opposition had been the team of the eighties, league champions two years earlier and runners-up the previous season but they weren't the Liverpool who had earned the club its superb reputation. Certainly they were a very good side but they'd finished sixth in the league, lost both legs of their UEFA Cup quarter-final to Genoa, been dumped out of the League (Rumbelows) Cup by Peterborough and had faced fewer top flight clubs en route to Wembley than Sunderland. Indeed Liverpool had only got to the final by beating second division Portsmouth on penalties in a semi-final replay. If only Pompey had won that shoot-out Sunderland would have had a massive chance at Wembley.

As the lowest-placed club to reach the cup final since Leicester City in 1949, Sunderland were very much the underdogs. The Lads had often thrived on that tag in the past but this time they were second best and Liverpool deserved to win.

Having been caretaker/manager since before Sunderland's opening game in the FA Cup, Malcolm Crosby had finally had the

John Byrne scored in every round except the final.

caretaker part of his title removed ten days before the final since when he'd overseen a pair of 2-2 draws. The team had been subject to constant change because quite apart from injuries, the cup tied-Don Goodman had been in and out of the side. There was a surprise to the cup final line-up though with the news that defender Paul Hardyman would be on the bench. He had started all seven games of the cup run and it was a double disappointment for the player who had missed Sunderland's previous visit to Wembley two years earlier because of suspension. He'd come on but never play for the club again. Also missing was cult hero John Kay, out through injury: "I had a calf strain. It was just wear and tear and I'd been struggling with it in the league. We had a lot of games shortly before the cup final and I tore it at Brighton," Kay explains.

Indeed Sunderland had squeezed nine league games in between the semi and the final but unlike 1973 they'd at least had a clear week to prepare. Gary Owers took over at right back and although he had a poor game in an attacking sense, could be proud of the fact that Liverpool only took over when man of the match Steve McManaman switched onto the other flank in the second half even though Sunderland tried to contain him by detailing Gordon Armstrong to help left back Anton Rogan. Doubling up Kerr and Malone on winger Eddie Gray had worked a treat in 1973 but in 1992 McManaman was unstoppable.

Sunderland put up a good show in the first half especially when you consider there were 33 league places between the clubs' final league positions. The Wearsiders got forward at every opportunity, prompted by captain Paul Bracewell. It was Brace's fourth FA Cup final and the ex Evertonian's third against Liverpool. Never renowned for his goalscoring, he at least came close to scoring only to be frustrated as his goalbound effort was deflected inches wide. It was to be the final game of his second spell at Sunderland. Controversially the Sunderland captain signed for Newcastle in the summer, the Magpies having offered him a two year contract rather than the 12 month deal Sunderland had on the table. Three years later he would return as player/assistant manager.

Sunderland's chief hope of a goal came in the form of John Byrne. He was seeking to become only the 10th player in history to score in every round, a select list that included Frank O'Donnell, who'd scored against Sunderland for Preston in the 1937 final. Byrne had scored seven goals in the cup run – the same number he'd managed in the league but the Republic of Ireland international, who was without a goal since the semi-final, saw his cup touch desert him. One decent first-half chance came Byrne's way but sadly he was unable to accept it.

Nonetheless at the interval Sunderland could be pleased with how they'd matched Liverpool and the dream was still alive. Just two minutes into the second half though Liverpool took the lead. "Michael Thomas lashed one in from distance that arrowed perfectly into the top corner," was how goalkeeper Tony Norman saw it. He'd done so much to get Sunderland to Wembley, but like Chris Turner in 1985 could do nothing to prevent defeat in the final.

Once Liverpool got their nose in front they never looked like relinquishing their lead and they got their nose even further in front when Ian Rush added a second in the 68th minute. It was Rush's fifth goal in an FA Cup final, a new record. "Rushie just slotted one in. He had the knack and I only know that because I trained with him with the Welsh national team," reflects Norman.

Thankfully Liverpool were content at 2-0. Had they wanted to they could probably have added another goal. Certainly they looked more likely to add to their tally than Sunderland looked like reducing it. It was Sunderland's fourth game beneath the Twin Towers in seven years and they hadn't scored, despite having penalties in two of them (including the 1988 League Centenary game lost on penalties to Wigan).

For Liverpool, it was the only trophy they would collect in the three-year tenure of manager Graeme Souness. Recovering from a heart bypass operation, Souness attended the game accompanied by his doctor with Ronnie Moran leading the men from Anfield out.

As runners-up Sunderland went up to get their medals first. It was only after collecting them they realised they'd been given the winners' medals by mistake. They had to swap them with the Liverpool players... so near yet so far.

v Sheffield United 2-0

Stadium of Light, play-off semi-final second leg (Sunderland win 3-2 on agg). May 13th 1998. Attendance: 40,092

SUNDERLAND	SHEFFIELD UNITED	REFEREE
Perez	Tracey	Mr. M. Pierce,
Holloway	Wilder	Portsmouth
Gray	Quinn	
Clark	Ford (Dellas)	
Craddock	Sandford	
Williams	Holdsworth	
Summerbee	Saunders	
Ball	Marker (Stuart)	
Quinn	Devlin	
Phillips (Dichio)	Marcelo (Morris)	
Johnston	Hamilton	
Unused subs: Ord,		
Rae		

SUNDERLAND'S FIRST game of the season having moved to the Stadium of Light was against Sheffield United. That match had been lost at Bramall Lane but the Lads had settled so smoothly into their new ground that after a moderate start they'd clearly been the best team in the league.

Only three games had been lost since a 'Nightmare on Elm Park' at Reading on October 4th while champions Forest had been comprehensively outplayed and beaten 3-0 on their own patch five months to the day later. However having climbed into an automatic promotion place for the last month of the season, a late slip up at Ipswich had condemned the Lads to the play-offs. Sunderland had 90 points, the highest ever achieved by a team not being promoted.

Consequently it had been a case of 'Back to the Future' at Bramall Lane for the first leg of the play-offs. The Blades had a decent team whose own promotion ambitions had been sidetracked by a run to the FA Cup semi-final and they'd already helped to produce the best match yet seen at the Stadium of Light. Sunderland had beaten

Sheffield 4-2 in January in a thrilling game that featured three goals in the final nine minutes.

United had undergone two changes of manager during the season but Steve Thompson's side came to the Stadium of Light with a 2-1 advantage. Kevin Ball had scored a great goal to put Sunderland ahead but United had fought back with second-half strikes from their Brazilian Marcelo and Greek defender Vassilis Borbokis.

Allan Johnston

The visitors had to make two changes for the return leg and were without goalscorer Borbokis. What was worrying though was that they only needed a draw and were away draw specialists. In all four divisions only Northampton could match their dozen away stalemates and to that they could add four away draws in the cups.

There was good news for Sunderland though with the return of Niall Quinn in place of Danny Dichio while a second change saw Michael Gray come in for Chris Makin. Backed by a Stadium of Light crowd that showed that while Roker Park might have been left behind, the 'Roker Roar' was still there, Sunderland tore into Sheffield.

Sunderland possessed a pair of brilliant wingers in Nick Summerbee and Allan Johnston. Each supplied the bullets for the

Lionel Perez dives in amongst the boots.

front two of Quinn and Phillips to fire. Summerbee was all about gaining half a yard and finding Quinn with an instantly delivered cross while 'Magic' Johnston preferred to leave his full back requiring the trainer to untie his legs after the Scot had tied them in knots. Johnston liked to jink inside and out and it was from such a run that Sunderland scored.

Twenty-one minutes were on the clock when Johnston's shot took a deflection off Nicky Marker as keeper Simon Tracey looked on forlornly. Sunderland were flying and Tracey would be overworked as the home side piled on the pressure for another goal.

Kevin Phillips was in his first season at Sunderland. He'd scored two late goals against Sheffield United on their league visit and needed just one more goal to equal Brian Clough's postwar record of 34 goals in a season. Superkev was unstoppable and on 38 minutes found the back of the net. It was his 16th goal in his last 15 appearances at the Stadium of Light. Brilliant.

Sunderland had led at half-time in the first leg too but the Blades had come back to win. Now the Lads again had a slender advantage and needed to hold it if they were to keep their promotion hopes alive with a trip to Wembley. This new ground – the biggest built in England in the second half of the twentieth century – had not been built for second-class football. From the visitors' point of view they'd already scored twice at Sunderland that season and if they could repeat the feat it could be them planning a trip to the capital.

United came at Sunderland in the second half, they had nothing to lose and gave Peter Reid's team a thorough examination. Standing as Sunderland's last line of defence was flamboyant French goalkeeper Lionel Perez. As Sheffield United threw everything they could at Sunderland, Perez produced the best save seen at the Stadium of Light to date and indeed the best save by a Sunderland goalkeeper since Jim Montgomery's at Wembley in 1973. Like Monty's it was a double stop.

Paul Devlin smacked what seemed an unstoppable shot which Perez unbelievably got to. Whereas Monty had seen the rebound from his first save fall at the feet of Peter Lorimer, Lionel looked up to see Welsh international Dean Saunders meeting the ball with an open goal to shoot at. Saunders must have thought he'd scored but unbelievably Perez got in the way and kept it out. Just as Leeds United had known they'd never score at Wembley, so Sheffield United knew nothing was going past this chap on this night. Their fightback faded, and Sunderland were through.

It proved to be Perez's final game at the Stadium of Light but what a way to go out. He said afterwards: "It is hard to describe the strength the fans give me. What an atmosphere. At the beginning of the game I thought, 'Nothing can happen to me here. You don't have to be afraid of anything with these people. They are with you.' "

v Charlton Athletic 4-4

Wembley, play-off final
May 25th 1998. Attendance: 77,739

SUNDERLAND	CHARLTON ATH	REFEREE
Perez	Ilic	Mr. E.K. Wolstenholme,
Holloway (Makin)	Mills (Robinson)	Blackburn
Gray	Bowen	
Clark (Rae)	Jones K.	
Craddock	Rufus	
Williams	Youds	
Summerbee	Newton	
Ball	Kinsella	
Quinn	Bright (Brown)	
Phillips (Dichio)	Mendonca	
Johnston	Heaney (Jones S)	

ASK NEUTRALS to pick the most famous post war-Wembley matches and arguably Sunderland would be the only team other than England to feature more than once. England 3-6 Hungary, England 9-3 Scotland, England 4-2 West Germany, Blackpool 4-3 Bolton, Man Utd 4-1 Benfica, Sunderland 1-0 Leeds and Sunderland 4-4 Charlton. Try coming up with a game good enough to knock any of those magnificent seven out of the top spots.

The 1998 play-off final with Charlton was a sensational game that, not content with eight goals, then had fourteen pen- alties for the richest prize in world football –

Manager Peter Reid.

promotion to the cash laden English top flight. For Sunderland supporters though, a scrappy game that had the uncommitted dozing off in front of their TV screens would have been better if only Sunderland had won. Typical Sunderland, go to Wembley score ten times and still lose.

Arriving at Wembley ages before kick-off it was nigh on impossible to spot a Charlton fan, the Addicks eventually ambling up on the tube from South London shortly before the game whereas the Wearside exodus had been going on all night.

Charlton were a decent team who played good football. They'd only finished two points behind Sunderland and both league fixtures had ended all square. Alan Curbishley's men had good reason to be confident. They hadn't conceded a goal in nine matches of which they'd won eight. Since Kevin Phillips scored against them in a 1-1 draw at the Valley 71 days earlier the only team to score against them were eventual champions Forest who they'd hammered 4-2.

At 0-0 Phillips was clean through only to be thwarted by a dubious offside decision. In the 21st minute Kevin Ball put a header from a corner over the top only for Charlton to grab the important opening goal two minutes later through Clive Mendonca. Charlton fans had good reason to believe their defence would see them to the Premiership and when they reached half-time without too much trouble that feeling would have been reinforced. Meanwhile in the Sunderland dressing room, manager Peter Reid was replacing full back Darren Holloway with Chris Makin, a move which centre forward Niall Quinn feels changed the game: "Chris is a passer of the ball, a cultured full back. We suddenly started getting the ball, passing it around and we found our way. We started to open Charlton up and I have to say it was the most enjoyable 45 minutes I've ever played in. We absolutely controlled the game, played some lovely football and had people on the edge of their seats."

Within five minutes of the restart Quinn equalised, bulleting the ball into the net having got across his marker Eddie Youds. It was exactly 900 minutes since Charlton had conceded. It would only be a further eight until they conceded again and in between Niall put a Lee Clark-created chance over the bar. It was Superkev who put Sunderland ahead but the goal was made by the other Superkev in the team, Kevin Ball. Bally thundered into a 50-50 with Keith Jones and as usual in a 50-50 it would be Ball who would win it, on this occasion sending Phillips straight through. "I dived in for a header where the boots were flying and got a whack on the head, but that didn't matter when I saw Kevin Phillips latch onto my pass and go on and score," says Bally. Phillips still had some work to do but held off Mark Bowen before expertly lobbing the Charlton keeper. The goal was Sunderland's 100th of the season in all competitions and meant Phillips had broken Brian Clough's post-war seasonal goal-scoring record with his 35th of the campaign. Unfortunately Phillips would only last another quarter of an hour. If he'd been able to stay on might Sunderland have won?

At this point Sunderland were playing like a team from the league they were trying to get into but those hopes plunged again in the 71st minute when Mendonca scored again. Receiving from Keith Jones, the striker took the ball past Darren Williams and found the back of the net. It was all happening now though and Quinn had Sunderland ahead again within two minutes, chesting down Clark's ball in and swivelling to beat keeper Sasa Ilic to make it 3-2 with 17 minutes left.

Sunderland then had the opportunity to take a two-goal lead, something neither team enjoyed all afternoon. The chance fell to substitute Danny Dichio, just on for Phillips. Had Summerbee's cross fallen to Phillips it would have been 'Goodnight Ilic' if not quite 'Goodnight Irene' but Dichio scuffed his attempted volley and Irene could have saved it, never mind Ilic.

Given a lifeline Charlton continued to press. Perez came out and comfortably took a corner but soon afterwards conceded another with a reflex save to deny Mark Bright. Bright would have his revenge. As the corner came over, Bright blocked Perez's route to the ball leaving the keeper unable to either get to the cross he'd gone for or be in position to deal with an effort on goal. The flag kick was met by Richard Rufus. The centre back had made his full league debut in 1994 at Roker Park...and had never scored – until now.

Sunderland had had the game almost won. The task now was to try and win it again. Nine minutes into extra time Michael Gray came forward as he'd been doing effectively all season. He played a diagonal pass into Quinn and from his neat lay-off Nick Summerbee put Sunderland 4-3 up. For a moment many wondered was it a 'Golden Goal?' It certainly would have been the most golden of goals but sadly for Sunderland the 'Golden Goal' rule wasn't being used.

It was the third time Sunderland had led but to Charlton's credit

Niall Quinn celebrates.

for the third time they came back, this time with a third goal for Clive Mendonca. The striker was London born but raised in Sunderland. He wasn't about to visit friends on Wearside for a while, especially not after his 'machine gun' celebrations.

Out on their legs, both sides pushed for yet another goal in the second half of extra time which proved to be the only section of play without a goal as the match incredibly finished four all.

Sunderland had won five of the six penalty shoot-outs they'd ever taken part in up to this point. Beginning with a 7-6 League Cup triumph at Newcastle in 1979, the only reverse had been at Manchester City in a Full Members' Cup tie that no one would lose sleep over. Lose this one and there'd be many, many sleepless nights ahead.

The penalties were at the Sunderland end with Charlton going first. Mendonca, Brown, Jones K., Kinsella and Bowen expertly converted Charlton's first five with Summerbee, Johnston, Ball, Makin and Rae all scoring for Sunderland. Two of the three players who Peter Reid had had to take off would have been good candidates for spot kick duty – Phillips and Clark – but after Robinson scored

Chris Makin

the first 'sudden-death' penalty for Charlton up stepped Quinn to take the first senior penalty of his career. Niall duly obliged to add a shoot-out penalty to his two goals.

Shaun Newton maintained Charlton's 100% record with their seventh penalty. Still to take one for Sunderland, apart from the keeper, were centre backs Craddock and Williams, left back Gray and sub Dichio. Sunderland-born Gray volunteered. His only previous penalty had been in the League Cup at Liverpool two seasons earlier. It had been easily saved. So was this one.

Sunderland were beaten 7-6 on penalties. Gray was inconsolable but no one blamed the lad. He'd had the bottle to take one and he had the bottle to come back and be nothing short of superb the following season, being part of a side that strolled the league and forcing himself into the England team.

As footballing disappointments go it was right down there with Gillingham in 1987, a reminder of that match being Keith Peacock: Gillingham manager in the '87 play-off and now part of the Charlton backroom team.

Kevin Ball at home with his play-off final shirt.

How did the fans react to such deep disappointment? Did they run on the pitch or wreck Trafalgar Square? Of course not, they showed their class as they had at the 'Friendly Final' with Norwich at Wembley in 1985. In a book produced by Charlton called *From Welling to Wembley* celebrating their club's famous victory one contributor writes: "After the match I was completely drained – and we had won! Heaven knows what the Sunderland supporters felt like. Then something happened that I had never experienced before that sealed a perfect day. As I left the stadium there were still hundreds of Sunderland fans moving along the concourse. They saw us, stopped and began applauding, wishing us luck for next season."

For Sunderland nothing would depend on luck next time round. Peter Reid, Niall Quinn and Kevin Ball got hold of the players, got their heads up and promised to win promotion next year. Easily said but a record 105 points the following season showed that it wasn't just fantastic support that Sunderland had.

v Bury 5-2

Gigg Lane, New Division One
April 13th 1999. Attendance: 8,669

SUNDERLAND	BURY	REFEREE
Sorensen	Kiely	Mr.F. G. Stretton,
Makin	West	Nottingham
Gray	Serrent	
Ball (Holloway)	Daws	
Melville	Lucketti	
Butler	Woodward	
Summerbee	Swailes	
Clark	Lilley	
Quinn (Dichio)	D'Jaffo	
Phillips	Bullock	
Johnston (Bridges)	Billy	
	Unused subs: Foster,	
	Littlejohn, Barnes	

THE 1998-99 season was one long procession to the promotion coronation. Recovering from the play-off final defeat on penalties, Peter Reid's side simply started as they meant to go on, and didn't stop. The first five games brought four wins and a draw, the season as a whole just three defeats meaning that only six league games out of 82 were lost. The Lads simply carried all before them, despite losing Kevin Phillips for three months due to injury. Sunderland had never been off the top of the table since Bury were beaten at the Stadium of Light in October. Now with 15 points still to play for Sunderland could mathematically wrap up promotion although so wide was the winning margin that Sunderland could have lost at Bury and the following four games and still finished top. Bury boss Neil Warnock had said in October that Sunderland would win the league by 15 points. Sunderland were better than that – they won it by 18 points.

Away fans had been given three sides of the ground as Bury became the latest club to welcome the red and white army providing them with their biggest gate of the season in front of a live TV audience. It was familiar territory for Peter Reid in more ways than

Kevin Phillips scored four times at Bury's Gigg Lane.

one. He and his brother had played for Bury and he'd taken Sunderland to promotion three years earlier.

The Lads didn't hang about, Phillips opening the scoring from the penalty spot in the 11th minute. Bury had everything to play for as they grappled with the threat of relegation and the Shakers shook Sunderland with a tremendous 23rd-minute equaliser from Darren Bullock.

Sunderland didn't mess about in this season of seasons. They achieved more points than any team ever had in any division and they did that in style. Bury were level for less than a minute, Niall Quinn restoring the lead with his 20th goal of the season. Before half-time Phillips had put his claim on the match ball by completing his hat-trick with two goals in three minutes just past the half hour, the first of which was Sunderland's 100th goal of the season in all competitions. At 4-1 Sunderland didn't have one foot in the Premiership, virtually the whole body was there with maybe just a trailing foot still to step over the line. That was only 45 minutes away.

Nick Daws pulled a goal back for Bury 20 minutes after the restart, giving his side the distinction of being the only team to score

Chris Makin

more than once against Sunderland in their 17-match unbeaten run to the close of the season. Despite being hauled back to 2-4, the visitors were never anything but in full control and in the final minute Kevin Phillips gave the nation another taste of what the next season's Premiership top scorer looked like by curling in a brilliant shot for Sunderland's fifth and his own fourth of the evening. It was the first time Sunderland had scored five goals away from home in a league match for almost exactly 35 years and they picked a perfect night to do so.

Many Bury fans had the good grace to stay for Sunderland's lap of honour on what was a fabulous night especially after the previous season's disappointment. Now, for the first time since the club moved to the Stadium of Light, Sunderland were back in the big time.

In the away dressing room a Nationwide League sign had been erected as the backdrop for the TV interviews. Sunderland weren't in that league any more though and an exuberant Niall Quinn demolished it. "It's true that after the match I smashed up the sign in our dressing room that proclaimed 'Nationwide League' and said a few things about how pleased I was to be out of it. The people from the Nationwide wrote to me," says Niall. "I had to write back and apologise."

Three days later, with a point needed to mathematically guarantee the championship, the Lads won 3-1 at Barnsley with another great goal from Phillips.

v Newcastle Utd 2-1

St. James' Park, Premier League
August 25th 1999. Attendance: 36,420

SUNDERLAND	NEWCASTLE UTD	REFEREE
Sorensen	Wright	Mr. G. Poll,
Makin	Barton	Hertfordshire
Gray	Goma	
Bould	Dabizas	
Butler	Domi	
Summerbee	Solano	
Rae	Dyer	
Schwarz (Ball)	McClen	
McCann	Speed	
Quinn	Maric (Shearer)	
Phillips	Robinson (Ferguson)	
Unused subs: Oster,	*Unused subs:* Harper,	
Marriott, Dichio,,	Green, Hughes	
Helmer		

NEWLY PROMOTED Sunderland went into their fifth game of the season three points better off than Newcastle but yet to pick up a point away from home. On a night of torrential rain Sunderland came from behind to seal a famous victory and leave Newcastle fans so desperate for an excuse that the weather was to blame – apparently.

Given how wet it was Newcastle might have expected to get more out of their subs and indeed their choice of subs was a major talking point. Magpie manager Ruud Gullit had both Alan Shearer and Duncan Ferguson on the bench. In Ferguson's case he was coming back from injury while Shearer had missed Newcastle's previous game through suspension. The Tynesiders had scored three goals and collected their first point of the season in that match and Gullit kept faith with young Sunderland supporting and Sunderland-born striker Paul Robinson.

For all the talk of Newcastle's much vaunted strike force there could be no argument that Sunderland's was better. Phillips alone scored more than Shearer and Ferguson put together that season

Kevin Ball

while Quinn added 14 of his own. Superkev became the only Englishman to ever win the European Golden Shoe as Europe's top scorer... and both would score this night to give Sunderland a famous victory.

Both of Sunderland's front two threatened early on at the Gallowgate End but Newcastle soon started to enjoy the majority of play as the home side. As usual Gary Speed, that fine midfield player, started to become a real influence and Robinson's willing running was always likely to test a Sunderland central defence of Bould and Butler who were probably more adept at dealing with Shearer and Ferguson.

After 28 minutes Newcastle went ahead when Robinson fed Kieron Dyer who broke clear to beat Thomas Sorensen. The black and whites were to hold the lead until 19 minutes into the second half but the break signalled a sea-change as Sunderland played with the tide in the second half.

With good footballers in midfield in Stefan Schwarz, Alex Rae and Gavin McCann, and a goal-maker in Nick Summerbee on the right wing, Sunderland came out ready to take the game to the Tynesiders. Just short of the hour mark Gullit withdrew Robinson for Ferguson with the clear intention of banging more long balls up to the big Scot as he sensed Sunderland now had the upper hand in the centre of the park.

The substitution failed to stem the red and white flow as in the 64th minute Sunderland got the leveller they'd been threatening. Predictably it was created by the boot of Summerbee. The winger took a free kick from wide on the right. As the ball squirted in, Quinn had to stoop slightly as he came to meet it, expertly re-directing the cross by glancing it goalwards and using the pace that was already on the ball. Niall Quinn was a brilliant centre forward and this was a brilliant goal. Quinny made it look easy – that was part of his talent.

Having got the goal Sunderland were all over Newcastle, the 800 Sunderland fans allowed in were doing their Gene Kelly impersonations while the home fans quivered, seeing through their fingers the 'ghosts' of Gates and Gabbiadini in Quinn and Phillips. Sunderland had a front two to frighten them again and their nerves were jangling more than a Morris dancing convention.

Peter Reid sent on Kevin Ball to rattle them even more and three minutes later Gullit sent Shearer on, much to the delight of the home fans. Before the Tyneside talisman could make an impression though he found his team 2-1 down.

Once again Summerbee was the architect, playing a great ball through for Phillips to run onto and burst clear of the home defence. Newcastle's on loan goalkeeper Tommy Wright was playing the first game of his second spell with the club and stood up well to block Superkev's shot. The Magpies thought they'd got away with it but Phillips chased the rebound, kept his balance as he spun round as if he was on a jet-ski and chipped the keeper with a perfectly weighted shot. Wright was powerless to stop the ball as it looped over him and dropped so beautifully into the Geordies' net.

So used to having the upper hand in the last half dozen years during which they'd flirted with success and played Champions League football while spending zillions, Newcastle were being made to realise that it was Sunderland's turn to be the dominant force in north east football once again.

Kevin Ball loved it more than anyone; he may be from Hastings but he is as red and white as they come, but Bally nearly blew it. Deep in injury time it looked as if there'd be one more injury when in typical fashion he threw himself into a challenge with Ferguson 30 yards away from Sorensen's goal. Ferguson saw him coming and tried to jump out of the way as the ball ricocheted towards the Sunderland goal. Sorensen got the feeling Wright had when Phillips scored but thankfully the ball hit the bar rather than dropping into the back of the net. It had been a storm of biblical proportions and it seemed there was a God after all.

Three days later Ruud Gullit resigned.

v Chelsea 4-1

Stadium of Light, Premiership
December 4th 1999. Attendance: 41,199

SUNDERLAND	CHELSEA	REFEREE
Sorensen	De Goey	Mr. S. Dunn,
Makin	Lambourde	Bristol
Gray	Babayaro	
Thirlwell	Morris	
Craddock	Hogh	
Williams	Desailly (Terry)	
Summerbee (Holloway)	Harley (Goldbaek)	
Schwarz	Poyet	
Quinn	Flo	
Phillips	Zola	
Roy	Wise (Wolleaston)	
Unused subs: Marriott,	*Unused subs:* Cudicini,	
Butler T, Oster,	Petrescu	
Reddy		

"**G**REATEST DAY in Decades" ran the *Football Echo*'s headline. Sunderland absolutely slaughtered Chelsea with football that was the pinnacle of the Peter Reid years and the Quinn / Phillips partnership, each of them scoring twice.

What made it even better was that Chelsea had hammered Sunderland 4-0 on the opening day of the season. Being the Lads' first game after the 105-point promotion it was a rude awakening to the Premiership particularly as 4-0 didn't begin to tell the tale. It could have been 14 as Poyet and Zola looked like players from another planet. Since then though Sunderland had quickly got to grips with the big boys, especially after the belief bestowed on the team following the win at Newcastle. When Chelsea rolled up at the Stadium of Light, fourth-placed Sunderland were above them in the table.

Just 44 seconds into the game, the Lads were one up. French midfielder Eric Roy, on his best performance for Sunderland, gave Niall Quinn a very early chance which he gleefully accepted. That set the tone as Chris Makin and Nick Summerbee caused havoc down

Superkev celebrates his screamer against Chelsea.

the right and Mickey Gray's overlapping down the left constantly stretched an overworked visiting defence who survived an appeal for a stonewall penalty when Roy was brought down.

Come the 23rd minute and the best goal yet seen at the 63-game old Stadium of Light arrived. ITV's *The Premiership* highlights programme used it on its opening titles for the following season and right up there with the 'chip in the rain' at St. James' it still stands as the best of Kevin Phillips' 130 goals that made him Sunderland's top post-war goalscorer. Superkev was fully 30 yards out when he leathered one that screamed into the top corner. It climaxed a period of play when Sunderland had made Chelsea look second rate. "Sunderland played magnificently for 45 minutes...we were outplayed with and without the ball," said Chelsea manager Gianluca Vialli graciously afterwards.

By now the crowd were in raptures. 'Was it like this when my granddad was watching Raich Carter?' people must have been wondering. Everyone on Wearside has been brought up on tales of Carter, Gallacher, Shack and Charlie Hurley. Now people were watching the players and a game they'd be telling their grandchildren about. "Quinn and Phillips, man, now you're talking!"

The front two had both scored and both would score again before half-time. Chelsea centre back Marcel Desailly had won a World Cup winners' medal the previous year but couldn't handle Quinn, eventually going off to be

Eric Roy

replaced by a young John Terry. A month earlier England centre back Sol Campbell had had a similarly dreadful time as Quinn scored twice in a home win over Tottenham. The Irishman was irrepressible. On 36 minutes Dutch goalkeeper Ed de Goey did well to parry a Quinn shot but fell to the ground looking like a drowning man watching the last lifeboat leave as Phillips was there in a flash to net the loose ball. Two minutes later there was Quinn again, volleying home the fourth goal.

All this was at the South End of the stadium, right in front of the Chelsea fans, who 38 minutes earlier had been reminding the home crowd of the score at Stamford Bridge. Suddenly they weren't so keen on chanting '4-0'.

Sunderland had gone into the game missing four players but the replacements slotted in so you couldn't see the join. One of them was the home-grown central midfielder Paul Thirlwell who was making his first top flight appearance. "To take part in a match like that was unbelievable," he said. "I couldn't believe it when we went in at half-time four up but I don't think anybody could say we didn't deserve it. We should have had a penalty and if we had scored six I don't think Chelsea could have argued. We knew we would struggle to keep up that level of performance in the second half but the gaffer told us to go out and keep the pressure on them and not let them settle into any rhythm and that's what we did."

Chelsea got a consolation goal through Gus Poyet nine minutes from time as Sunderland saw out a game won within 38 minutes on one of the club's finest days. "The players certainly did the club proud with their performance against Chelsea and we've received a tremendous amount of correspondence and a lot of well wishes from supporters saying it was the best first 45 minutes they had ever seen," noted manager Peter Reid in his programme notes at the next home game.

It was Sunderland's biggest home win in the top flight since the week after the club's joint record defeat in 1982.

v Newcastle Utd 2-1

St. James' Park, Premiership
November 18th 2000. Attendance: 52,030

SUNDERLAND	NEWCASTLE UTD	REFEREE
Sorensen	Given	Mr. G. Poll,
Makin (Arca)	Solano	Tring,
Gray	Domi	Hertfordshire
Thome	Caldwell	
Craddock	Hughes	
Hutchison	Lee	
Williams	Dyer	
Rae	Acuna (Barton)	
Kilbane	Shearer	
Quinn (Dichio)	Bassedas (Lua Lua)	
Phillips	Speed	
Unused subs: Macho,	*Unused subs:* Harper,	
Varga, Oster	Griffin, Cordone	

NEWCASTLE HAD spent over a year seething with indignation. They'd been beaten at home by Sunderland the previous season and then led 2-0 at the Stadium of Light in the return only to end up drawing. This time they were going to put the Mackems in their place and show them who was boss. Since Sunderland's visit the previous season a ground extension had been opened meaning that now visiting supporters were so high up in the 'gods' that it was allegedly a quarter of a mile from the back row to the goal at the other end.

The home side now had Bobby Robson in charge rather than Ruud Gullit and their South American players had apparently been given lessons about the importance of the clash. Sunderland's own South Americans needed no such guidance; Brazilian Emerson Thome and Argentinian Julio Arca were well attuned to the area and playing for Peter Reid there was never anyone in the team if they weren't totally committed.

Tyneside frustration was unleashed as the referee blew for kick-off. Within 20 seconds Speed had the goal at his mercy as Sunderland parted like the Red Sea but he panicked and shot well wide. Before four minutes were on the clock though the same player had found the back of the net. Receiving from Solano, the Welshman scored at the second attempt. His header had come back off the post, inadvertently struck Don Hutchison and landed back at his feet. Speed was on the ground when he hit his shot but every other black and whiter in the ground was on their feet as the net rippled.

Only two more minutes had passed when Acuna headed into the side netting as the Magpies swooped around the Sunderland penalty area. Lesser teams would have crumbled beneath the onslaught but as any Sunderland player looked around his teammates he wouldn't have been able to find a 'bottler'. The likes of Makin, Craddock, Williams and Rae might not have been world beaters but they could be counted on when things weren't going well and along with the entire team they simply put their tin helmets on, dug in and began the fightback.

Niall Quinn was the first to give the home side something to think about, his feather-like touch oozing calm in the frenetic match going on around him. He delicately lobbed former Sunderland loan keeper Shay Given who only just managed to tip the shot over the bar. Sunderland then should have had the most blatant of penalties, Alan Shearer hauling Jody Craddock back as he came in on a cross at the far post. Referee Mr. Poll declined the award.

Despite these threats, Newcastle were still on top and Sunderland keeper Thomas Sorensen was kept busy, one save from a Speed header being particularly important in keeping the score at just 1-0 when half-time came.

Sunderland had gone into the match in decent form. Although just 11th in the table at kick-off there had been just one defeat in 11 in league and cup. The Lads began to push Newcastle back and in the 66th minute introduced teenager Arca, making just his 10th appearance for the club but already a favourite with the fans. Within a minute Sunderland were level, the goal coming from local lad Don Hutchison. It came from a left wing cross from Kevin Phillips. Coming in on the far post, Hutchison took the chance expertly. It was

Thomas Sorensen saves Alan Shearer's penalty.

the third successive game he'd scored in and the jewel in the crown of the ten goals he scored in his only full season with the club.

The home fans were devastated. All that anger and ambition to beat Sunderland and despite their early goal here were the Wearsiders back on level terms two-thirds of the way through the game. Three minutes later they knew it wasn't their day when Solano hit the post with a free kick and then Sunderland really rubbed it in with the winner. Sunderland supporters would have been delirious if the goal had been as scrappy as Newcastle's but it was a brilliant goal, one that showed once again that when it came to centre forwards Niall Quinn was top man.

Sunderland-born Michael Gray was captain and created the goal. The move started right back with keeper Sorensen. Gray and Rae combined on Sunderland's left before Gray raced towards the Newcastle goal. Looking up he saw Quinn in the middle, as tall and proud as Souter Lighthouse. Hitting a high lofted cross on the run Gray signed and sealed with a note saying, 'Here's a gift for you Quinny, please head this one past Shay Given.' Niall's eyes lit up when he saw this peach of a cross coming his way. Timing his run perfectly he was at the apex of his jump when his 6'4" frame connected with the ball, sending it perfectly over Given and right into the very top corner of the Newcastle net. This is a book of Sunderland's greatest games. Sadly a book of Sunderland's games where the supporters spent loads of money, travelled the length of the country, saw a, shall we politely say 'disappointing' performance and trooped dejectedly back again would be a much bigger book. What makes it all worthwhile are moments like this. Priceless.

There was more to come. In his inimitable style Niall couldn't keep out of the headlines and with just a few minutes on the clock went sliding in on Shearer just inside the angle of the box. It was a centre forward's challenge and a definite penalty. The referee had no hesitation in quite rightly giving it although he'd been happy for Shearer to foul Craddock in the same box in the first half. A penalty it was though and as Shearer put the ball on the spot the home fans got ready to celebrate and consider would there be enough time for them to get a winner? Shearer got a lot of goals from the spot. This wouldn't be one of them.

Kevin Ball tells an amusing story of Thomas Sorensen insisting he had Ball's ricocheted block that hit the bar from 30 yards covered in the last minute of the previous season's win at St. James'. On this occasion there was no doubt that Sorensen had the spot kick well and truly covered. The keeper dived full length to his left, stretching every sinew and saved Shearer's penalty. The term 'Great Dane' could have been made for him there and then.

With the Newcastle fans stunned into silence, heads turned to a corner high up in the ground from which the chant, 'Shearer, Shearer' was emanating. Irony was lost on the home crowd but the Sunderland supporters were already contemplating what excuses the Magpies would have this time as it hadn't rained. There were none and they knew it. To have seen Sunderland win successive league derbies at Newcastle before you would have had to be there in 1932 and 1933. This was a victory to savour.

v Burnley 3-2

Stadium of Light, Championship
April 27th 2007. Attendance: 44,448

SUNDERLAND	BURNLEY	REFEREE
Ward	Jensen	Mr. T. Kettle,
Simpson	Duff	Berkshire
Collins	Harley	
Nosworthy	Thomas	
Evans	Caldwell	
Edwards	Elliott (Spicer)	
Whitehead	Djemba-Djemba	
Miller L. (Leadbitter)	McCann (Gudjonsson)	
Stokes (Hysen)	McVeigh	
Murphy	Jones (Akinbiyi)	
Connolly (John)	Gray	
Unused subs: Fulop,	*Unused subs:* Coyne,	
Yorke	Coughlan	

THIS THRILLING match all but sealed promotion under manager Roy Keane in what was Niall Quinn's first season after he returned to the club as chairman. As Carlos Edwards thundered home a late winner right out of the pages of *Roy of the Rovers*, Keane allowed himself a little hop and skip forward, a fist came briefly out of his right pocket and then just as quickly his emotions went into lockdown as a veneer of professionalism exuded from the charismatic manager. Inside Roy was as delighted as anyone but he knew the job wasn't quite finished yet. The live TV cameras switched to Quinn in the directors' box.

As Edwards' shot nestled in the top corner of the net, the chairman leapt out of his seat, eyes to the heavens as the moment his belief, his ability to get together a group of investors to take over and his passion for the club he'd fallen in love with came together, now within touching distance of its first tangible reward of promotion.

A few minutes later, when referee Kettle blew the final whistle, Sunderland knew that their destiny was in their own hands. Three points from the sole remaining game away to bottom-of-the-table

Luton would secure promotion. As it happened, Derby, the third team in a three horse race, lost at Crystal Palace two days later. Sunderland were duly promoted ahead of their 5-0 victory at Luton which also brought the Championship title ahead of Steve Bruce's Birmingham who slipped up at Preston.

Managed by former Sunderland assistant manager Steve Cotterill, who had endured an unhappy time as number two to Howard Wilkinson at the Stadium of Light in a five month spell either side of the turn of 2003, Burnley's side included two ex Sunderland players: Andy Gray and Steve Caldwell. The latter had headed the goal that had won promotion just two years earlier – only for Sunderland to be immediately relegated yet again. They also included Jon Harley who knew how the Stadium of Light could erupt – he'd been part of the Chelsea team 'an – niall – ated' in 1999.

Sunderland began the game positively and took a 14th-minute lead thanks to Daryl Murphy. Straight away there was a chance to further ease any nerves when the first of the game's three penalties was awarded. Top scorer David Connolly picked himself to take the spot kick after he'd gone down under the slightest of touches from Wayne Thomas only to see Burnley keeper Brian 'The Beast' Jensen save his shot.

Within a couple of minutes the visitors were level through a penalty of their own, neatly converted by Andy Gray (one debut goal in 22 appearances for Sunderland) to leave a game Sunderland needed to win delicately balanced. The Lads weren't playing at all badly but the visitors had risen to the challenge and were making it difficult. Played on a Friday night for TV, supporters of promotion hopefuls Birmingham and Derby – two points separated the top three – were all Burnley supporters for the night.

Those Birmingham and Derby fans were toasting the Claret and Blues five minutes into the second half when Wade Elliott beat Sunderland goalkeeper Darren Ward with a spectacular 25 yarder. Sunderland needed a goal just to rescue a point and a point wouldn't be good enough. If they lost or drew there was every chance

Carlos Edwards scores his stunning goal.

Sunderland would be condemned to the play-offs where their record was awful. The pressure was on.

Two minutes later came the third spot kick of the night. Having already had one saved Connolly could have been forgiven for stepping aside and letting someone else have a go but he grabbed the ball. Had he missed two penalties in a game of such importance he'd have had to live with that forever but showing all his experience the Republic of Ireland international kept his composure and scored. It must have been an enormous relief for Connolly but there was no 'Stuart Pearce' style releasing of frustrations, he just dashed into the back of the net, grabbed the ball, and raced back to the half-way line. Sunderland needed another goal and there were 38 minutes to get it.

To their credit, Burnley continued to offer stiff resistance and those 38 minutes had shrunk to just 11 when Edwards' moment of magic arrived. It was a goal fit to win any game, the move starting one yard from Sunderland's goal line. Jonny Evans, on loan from Man Utd, began the move with an interception. He found Toby Hysen who swiftly laid it off to fellow substitute Grant Leadbitter. Another swift pass fed Daryl Murphy. He had opened the scoring and has to take a fair bit of the credit for this great goal. Bringing the ball across the half-way line, he cut across the pitch, spotted Edwards racing up the right flank into oceans of space, and rolled a perfectly weighted ball into the winger's path. The Trinidadian took a touch to steady himself and then fired in an absolute rocket from well outside the box. Edwards had scored screamers at Birmingham and Southampton but this was the pick of his own personal 'Goal of the Season competition'.

It was a fabulous goal, that said Premier League here we come. Sunderland were on their way.

v **Newcastle Utd** 2-1

Stadium of Light, Barclays Premier
League. October 25th 2008.
Attendance: 47,936

SUNDERLAND	NEWCASTLE UTD	REFEREE
Fulop	Given	Mr. M. Riley,
Chimbonda	Beye	
Ferdinand	Coloccini	
Collins	Taylor	
McCartney	Bassong (Enrique)	
Yorke (Jones)	Geremi (Gutierrez)	
Malbranque (Tainio)	Butt (Barton)	
Whitehead	Guthrie	
Richardson	Duff	
Diouf (Reid)	Ameobi	
Cisse	Martins	
Unused subs: Bardsley,	*Unused subs:* Capaca,	
Chopra, Leadbitter,	Harper, N'Zogbia,	
Colgan	Xisco	

SUNDERLAND HAVE had many great results but possibly only the long awaited first ever FA Cup triumph in 1937 after the league title had been claimed no fewer than six times has been dreamt of on Wearside for longer than this victory. Sunderland had not beaten their old rivals at home for 28 years. In that stretch of over quarter of a century since Stan Cummins' April 1980 Roker Park winner, rivalry between red and white and black and white supporters had taken on a new and not altogether welcome element. Those who 'support all the north east teams' were by 2008 an ever diminishing minority, people who had season tickets for both clubs were virtually extinct, victims partially of the ability to follow your side every weekend home and away brought about by greater affluence and the motorway network.

A generation of Sunderland supporters had grown up used to being the whipping boys in Wear-Tyne banter, taking the swipes of what they saw as the 'car-toon army' bragging about beating Barcelona in the Champions League while Sunderland were capable of losing to Barnsley all too often. Tyneside's entertainers of the Keegan era boasted glittering star names signed for astronomical amounts of money while Sunderland shopped for bargains and usually got what they paid for. Even Middlesbrough had a dazzling array of Brazilians and Italians, won their first ever trophy and reached a European final while Sunderland continued to mainly play second or even third fiddle interrupted only by a brief spell as top dogs in the Phillips-Quinn era. Those halcyon days brought two fabulous derby wins but both were at St. James', witnessed in the flesh only by the fortunate few to have tickets.

Newcastle had never lost at the Stadium of Light. They'd escaped with lucky draws more than once but there was no escape for the Magpies this time as they were soundly beaten by Roy Keane's rampant red and whites. French striker Djibril Cisse was to score in both derbies during the season, living up to his assertion in the match programme that "I've always scored on my derby days", the man on loan from Marseilles putting Sunderland one up in the 20th minute with an opportunist strike, turning in a ball screwed across the box from Steed Malbranque.

Sunderland had enjoyed the better of the opening 30 minutes but were pegged back on the half hour from a dead ball, Shola Ameobi losing his markers to head home a Geremi free kick at the far post. In doing so he beat goalkeeper Marton Fulop, making his first appearance of the season – and only his second ever top flight appearance – in for the injured regular choice Craig Gordon.

For the next 45 minutes Sunderland probed away looking to regain their advantage without success but just as the game ticked into its final quarter hour, with supporters beginning to wonder if the Tynesiders would once again name Harry Houdini as their man of the match, the Black Cats scored a goal truly fit to win a game of the greatest magnitude. El-Hadji Diouf did little in his half season as a Sunderland player but the Senegal international showed his experience by collecting the ball on the wing and exhibiting terrific closed control to drift infield and draw a foul from Nicky Butt right

Richardson's rocket. Kieran Richardson fires an
unstoppable shot into the Magpies' net.

on the edge of the box in a central position. Newcastle lined up a wall
Hadrian would have been proud of but it wasn't enough. Twenty-
eight years was far too long to wait. Thousands in the capacity crowd
hadn't been born the last time Sunderland scored a winning goal
against Newcastle on Wearside but these were the final few seconds.

Seven days earlier midfielder Kieran Richardson had bulleted a
free kick into Fulham's net at Craven Cottage only to see his effort
disallowed for an infringement in the wall and he'd also been
unlucky enough to see another free kick amazingly rebound off both
posts and the crossbar without going in but this was his moment.
Newcastle keeper Shay Given spent over a decade at Newcastle
winning less than the medal he'd won at Sunderland during a 17
game loan spell as a teenager and saw no more of Richardson's rocket
than he found silverware north of the Tyne.

As Kieran connected time seemed to stand still. Those 28 years
disappeared into the history books as the net bulged with the ferocity
of a shot unequalled at the Stadium of Light. It was as if every
supporter of Sunderland added their weight to the shot: "Once it left
my foot I knew it was in. I didn't really see it because it was so quick,"

said the scorer. "I got a good connection, was quite close to the goal and I think I had a bit of wind behind me. Once it went in I heard the biggest roar I've ever heard in my life and I knew how much it meant to the people and to give them that joy for that day was definitely one of the highlights of my career so far and I'm happy for that."

There was time for Cisse to hit the post but 2-1 was enough not just to win the game and reclaim the bragging rights but in the season's final analysis – with Newcastle being relegated two points behind Sunderland – the season was distilled in one game, even one moment. It was a moment that Wearside had waited and waited for and which had finally come not a moment too soon.

v Tottenham H 3-1

Stadium of Light, Barclays Premier
League. April 3rd 2010. Attendance: 43,184

SUNDERLAND	TOTTENHAM H	REFEREE
Gordon	Gomez	Mr. L. Mason,
Ferdinand	Walker	Lancashire
Richardson	Assou-Ekotto (Kranjcar)	
Turner	Kaboul	
Da Silva	Bassong	
Henderson	Bentley (Defoe)	
Meyler	Palacios	
Cattermole	Modric	
Malbranque (Zenden)	Bale	
Bent (Jones)	Pavlyuchenko (Crouch)	
Campbell (Bardsley)	Gudjohnsen	
Unused subs: Carson,	*Unused subs:* Alnwick,	
Kilgallon, Benjani,	Rose, Livermore,	
Liddle	Dervite	

S UNDERLAND'S HOME form in their first season under Steve
Bruce was good. Both Liverpool and Arsenal were beaten on
Wearside in the same season for the first time since 1954 and Spurs
too came a cropper when they came north sat nicely in fourth
position as they chased a Champions League berth. Sunderland were
unbeaten at home since before Christmas and relishing the visit of
Harry Redknapp's outfit. Sunderland had three former Spurs in their
line-up, all of whom would play key roles in the match.

No sooner had the game kicked off than it was time to kick off
again. Just 36 seconds had gone when Darren Bent scored right in
front of his former Spurs fans. It was a typical poacher's goal, Bent
being Johnny on the spot to net when Heurelho Gomes couldn't
hold a header from former Tottenham loan man Fraizer Campbell. It
was a terrific start: the earliest goal anyone scored in the Premier
League that season, the sixth fastest goal in Sunderland's history and
the second quickest ever seen at the Stadium of Light. The youthful
midfield trio of Lee Cattermole, Jordan Henderson and David Meyler

allowed Tottenham no time on the ball while wide on Sunderland's left, ex Tottenham maestro Steed Malbranque was the instigator of many of Sunderland's best moves. It was from a Malbranque shot just short of the half hour that Sunderland were awarded the first of their three penalties – the first time ever they had had three penalties in one match. Defender Kyle Walker handled the ball as a rebound from Gomes came back to him and referee Mason had no hesitation of pointing to the spot. Bent duly scored his second and had the chance of a hat trick before half-time from another spot kick in the 41st minute.

This time Croatian playmaker Luka Modric got his tackle on Campbell all wrong but Gomes rescued him when diving full length

Gomes makes a brilliant save from Bent's second penalty of the game.

to keep out Bent's penalty. The England striker had previously only failed to score from one penalty, his former teammate Gomes being the man to deny him in the earlier fixture at White Hart Lane. Bent was dynamite that season, finishing with 25 goals, all but one of them in the league. He became the first Sunderland player to get a goal for England since Shackleton in 1954 when he scored against Switzerland early the following season but astonishingly he was to have a second penalty saved against his former team.

Sunderland's third penalty of the game arrived just past the hour mark when Meyler was brought down. This time Bent blasted against the post with the keeper swooping on the rebound. Having had two great opportunities to wrap up the points there was always the fear that Spurs would get back into the game. The worry that Sunderland weren't getting the rewards for what was a scintillating display of football was reinforced three minutes later when Anton Ferdinand had a good-looking goal ruled out. The referee judged that Campbell had fouled the keeper a moment before Ferdinand fired home but the 'scorer' didn't realise. This was his 60th game for Sunderland and he thought it was his first goal. A huge fan of Michael Jackson who had died the previous year, Ferdinand had promised (threatened?) to celebrate the next goal he scored with a Michael Jackson-style 'moonwalk'. It may have been a series of small steps for Anton but he needed a giant leap back into position when he realised the game was about to restart with a free kick to Spurs.

Indeed the visitors did get back into the game and with a goal from a man who had declined a move to Sunderland at the start of the season. Beanpole Peter Crouch proved to be a 'Jack in the box' with a goal just one minute after coming on as a 71st-minute substitute.

At 2-1 with almost 20 minutes left and Redknapp's men with their tails up it had all the makings of another game to add to the list of games Sunderland should have won but threw away. It had been a thrilling game of the highest order, the home side being far superior on the day to a team destined to qualify for the Champions League with the end of the season just a month away. However the best moment was still to come.

With four minutes to go Jordan Henderson got away down Sunderland's right. Looking up, he picked out Boudewijn Zenden on the far side of the penalty area. The former Netherlands international had been on the pitch eight minutes. A veteran of a Champions League final and World Cup and European Championship semi-finals, Zenden had always been a player of the highest

Bolo Zenden scored an absolutely stunning volley.

class. As Henderson's high centre dropped to him, he arched his back, got his body into the perfect position and showing a level of skill only the very top players in the world can exhibit, he caught his volley absolutely brilliantly. Gomes may have saved two penalties but there was no way he was getting anywhere near this shot as it rocketed into the top corner. It was the most stunning goal to win a superb game and signal once again that under Steve Bruce Sunderland were a force to be reckoned with for any side stepping foot into the Stadium of Light.

BIBLIOGRAPHY

All the Lads, Garth Dykes & Doug Lamming, Polar, 2000
From Welling to Wembley, Anthony Fowles, Charlton Athletic F.C. 1998
Footballer's Progress, Raich Carter, Sporting Handbooks, 1950
Ha'way / Ho'way the Lads, Alan Candlish, Sports Books, 2006.
I Lead the Attack, Trevor Ford, Stanley Paul, 1957.
Left Back in Time, Len Ashurst, Know the Score, 2009.
PFA Premier & Football League Players' Records 1946-98, Barry J. Hugman.
    Queen Anne Press, 1998.
Soccer at War, Jack Rollin, Headline, 1985 & 2005.
Sunderland Cult Heroes, Rob Mason, Breedon, 2008.
Sunderland 'Match of My Life,' Rob Mason, Know The Score, 2006.
Sunderland's Number Ones, Rob Mason, Northdown, 1999.
Sunderland: The Complete Record, Rob Mason, Mike Gibson & Barry
    Jackson, Breedon 2005.
The Impossible Dream, Ian Porterfield with John Gibson, A.K.
    Publications, 1973
Rothmans and *Sky Sports* Year books. 1970-2010, Jack and Glenda Rollin.
Tottenham Hotspur, The official Illustrated History, Phil Soar, Ted Smart,
    1996
Plus match programmes from all available games, *Sunderland Echo*
    and *The Sunderland Football Echo*.